RETIREMENT: CREATING PROMISE

DATE DUE

MY 22 66	JE 23 0		
NO 1			
NO 20 8			
DE 11 81			
JE 18 91			
OC 6			
OC 8			
DE 16 06			

HQ1062
K54
c.2

1980

RETIREMENT

RETIREMENT

Creating Promise Out of Threat

Robert K. Kinzel

a division of american management associations

Library of Congress Cataloging in Publication Data

Kinzel, Robert K
    Retirement.

    Includes index.
    1. Retirement. 2. Retirement--United States.
I. Title.
HQ1062.K54   301.43'5   78-32165
ISBN 0-8144-5505-0

First Printing

To
Virginia

Author's Note

THE research for this book was conducted among males in middle or upper management. In virtually all cases, the opinions and feelings of the man's wife were sought, essentially to supplement the husband's point of view. I think that a retirement plan for women would make a very great contribution. The subject, however, is far too important and broad to be tucked into this book. Supported by the necessary research, I think it would be a worthwhile topic for my next book.

Robert K. Kinzel

Contents

1

Many Things to Many People

SOME of you are reading this book because you are about to retire and are apprehensive about doing so for one reason or another. Others of you are reading this book because you have retired already and are not entirely happy with the quality of your existence.

I have written this book because I think I have some things to tell you that may be useful. During my years as a management consultant, I assisted a great many people of many different backgrounds in the process of planning a satisfactory retirement. In addition, I have carried myself into the revised lifestyle of retirement, thereby receiving first-hand confirmation of my methods and perspectives.

At the outset, I want to say that nothing about retirement is a simple matter. However, retirement planning need not be overwhelming in its complexity. Much of the material written for retirees is condescending, almost insulting, as if readers were incapable of understanding what the writer had to say. This book begins with the premise that you are a competent individual, capable of solving problems, made wise by experience, and approaching retirement with many good years ahead.

Our sixty-fifth birthday would not have special significance if society had not made an arbitrary decision. It was Otto von Bismarck of Germany in the last century who established 65 as the age of retirement. At that time life expectancy was under 50, and most people who reached 65 were in poor health. Today life expectancy exceeds 70 years, and most people over 65 are still vigorous and active.

Nevertheless, retirement age has been declining in recent years, and the trend is for more and more people to seek earlier retirement. There are a number of reasons for this: improvements in financial status through social security benefits; longer pensions; technological changes that make skills obsolete; and the shorter workweek. All these changes have given people opportunities to seek a lifestyle other than working.

Recently retirement has been a subject of political concern, as evidenced by laws enacted by Congress to raise the mandatory retirement age to 70 for most workers. Raising or even eliminating the retirement age appeals to politicians, who are wooing the ever increasing number of people over 65. It also decreases the amounts to be paid out by the hard-pressed Social Security Administration.

There are already signs that this legislation is ill-conceived and will probably not, in the long run, reverse the trend toward early retirement. For example, many businesses are encouraging and training older employees for earlier retirement. The head of personnel in one large corporation told me his main job was to negotiate just and equitable retirement programs for over 250 employees under the age of 65.

Finally, a recent report from the Department of Labor suggests that any new legislation postponing or eliminating mandatory retirement will have limited effect and that the long-range trend toward early retirement will continue virtually unabated.

These issues affect a significant number of people. In 1960, about 16.5 million people were over the age of 65. In 1973, the number was over 20 million; in 1976, over 22 million. Today, more than 10 percent of the population is over 65 years old. (In 1900, only 4 percent of a much smaller population was over 65.)

According to estimates based on social security payments, well over 15 million of the 22 million people over 65 are retired. According to the Census Bureau, only 22 percent of men over 65 are still in the workforce. This does not mean that the ones who are working have the same jobs or make the same money as they did before. More likely it means that, because of their financial realities, they find it necessary to work at least part time.

Many of the stereotypes about retired people are dispelled when we look at the facts. For example, whether retirees continue to work or enjoy the benefits of capital accrued during the working years, five out of six have incomes above the poverty level designated by the federal government. Only 4 percent of the people over 65 are in retirement homes receiving so-called custodial care.

The Challenges of Retirement

Enforced retirement, with all its financial and social challenges, affects more people and a greater percentage of our population every year. No one can pretend that retirement is a simple matter, for it brings us to a major milestone in our lives, one that ranks in importance with finishing formal schooling, leaving home, and getting married. The impact on our lives and the challenge to our sense of well-being are dramatic. While there are physical and material concerns associated with retirement, the greatest stress appears to be in the social arena.

At every stage of life, including retirement, people must deal with the issues of survival and satisfaction. At the most basic level, of course, they must provide for their physical *subsistence.* Beyond that, they reach automatically for satisfactory ways of using their time that will enable them to achieve self-respect—a positive *self-image* that stems largely from the reactions of others. At the highest level of success in meeting life, people attain *self-satisfaction.*

This progress from subsistence to self-satisfaction forms a hierarchy of objectives first defined by Abraham Maslow.* I believe that it makes sense to approach these problems at any stage of life in sequential order.

In one way or another, retirement manages to overturn most of the solutions that a person has derived

---

* A. H. Maslow, "A Theory of Human Motivation," *Psychological Review,* July 1943, pp. 370–396.

from many years of living. At the very least, the solutions are called into question once again. New circumstances require new solutions. It is a matter of adjustment. Sometimes, the need to seek out new solutions produces almost unbelievable stress, even in people who generally have dealt with stress successfully in the past. This kind of stress can be paralyzing. It can produce an immobilizing fear.

When I started counseling people on retirement, I found over half my clients uncooperative about starting a plan (even when the corporation paid the fees). They simply didn't want to face retirement. When I asked what they might like to do, I got such answers as "I don't know," and "I'll face that problem after I'm retired and get settled." I realized I wasn't getting to first base with that approach, so I developed a procedure of starting with very specific, tangible aspects of financial planning to break the block. As you will see, that procedure is a very important part of this book.

Most likely, some of you have already experienced stress in looking forward to imminent retirement from the workforce. Although you know you should do so, you have not been able to analyze your situation, concentrate on your needs, and make constructive plans. *Be assured that you are not alone.* You're in very good company. Even decisive heads of industry have fallen prey to stress and immobility.

I once counseled a high-level executive in a large corporation who absolutely refused to consider what he was going to do when he retired. His stock reply to my questions was "I'll cross that bridge when I come to it." He managed to delay his retirement until he was 67, but even then he refused "to cross the bridge." He is obviously unhappy, but he still refuses to face reality and accept his new status. He has been seeking other jobs or part-time work without success, and is now vainly looking for a job as consultant.

Another powerful executive I know also retired without making plans. He impetuously sold his house and moved far away from his circle of friends. He did not make friends in the new community, and the stress made him quite ill. I finally convinced him to find something useful to do. He got fruitfully involved in an adult education program and now plays an important role in his community.

Rest assured, no one has to remain paralyzed. As you progress through this book, you will learn to think in interesting and nonthreatening ways about the special challenges that retirement presents to you.

Subsistence

Subsistence is the first and most important challenge you will have to deal with. You can scarcely free your mind to consider psychological and social matters until you have reassured yourself that you will have food, clothing, shelter, medical attention, and other basic requirements. This means that you are going to have to know quite clearly what your financial capability will be under a new set of circumstances. Perhaps you are looking forward to a time when future earnings from your work will be greatly limited or eliminated altogether. Maybe you have even tried to figure out, with some foreboding, just how long your present capital will last under various circumstances. There are many preliminary questions to consider before you can find the answers you need. In the next chapter, we will go through the steps of analyzing your financial circumstances and projecting your financial future as simply and painlessly as possible.

Self-Respect

Once you have a reasonably clear picture of your financial position, you can turn your attention to developing a lifestyle that will help you preserve your self-respect in retirement. Self-respect is derived from your standing in relation to family, friends, peers, and the community at large. Probably, you have been accustomed to an active, rather structured style of life. Your waking hours have been organized around working in an office, factory, or other location. A 40-hour week, plus the time involved in preparing for and traveling to and from work, leaves relatively little freedom for other activities. Most working people have barely enough time left over to deal with the logistics of shopping and chores. As retirement approaches, people inevitably begin to wonder: "What am I going to *do*—how will I keep busy—when I don't go to work anymore?"

Some people find that for financial or other reasons, or purely as a matter of preference, part-time work is a good idea. Frequently, however, part-time work is used as a means of avoiding the realities of retirement. Those who neither need nor want to work must find other ways to close the seemingly huge gaps in their day satisfactorily. Later in the book, we will return to this topic.

Even if you have so much money that financial needs are far from your mind, you still must be concerned with preserving your self-respect. The work ethic is very strong in our society. Traditionally, the breadwinner in a family places a very high value on his role. He receives respect and appreciation from others, and his self-respect is well supported. When he retires, many of his friends remain in the workforce. When they talk shop, what is he going to talk about? Sometimes, people experience a feeling of guilt when they are no longer getting up with the alarm clock and going to work. You must develop a satisfactory philosophy and plan to overcome this guilt feeling. At a purely practical level, you will have to make arrangements for spending time with the people you like. No one can afford to give up the feeling of belonging to a circle of friends.

When you retire you will also lose a certain amount of personal power over others—the kind of power that derives from your status on the job. The higher your position, the more power you will lose when you retire. This is most apparent with top executives, who have plenty of money but get their main satisfaction from the power of their positions. When such a loss occurs, and when people feel it to be important, new kinds of personal satisfactions must be found.

Self-Satisfaction

This leads us directly to the last major challenge to be faced in retirement. I refer to self-satisfaction, which goes beyond the attainment of self-respect. If others confer a positive self-image on you by showing you respect and making you feel that you belong, you are on the way to self-satisfaction. But more is required of you. Self-satisfaction can be achieved only if your life in retirement includes one or more carefully chosen, affirmative programs. You need to thrust yourself into activities so worthwhile to you that they are rewarding in themselves. The exact nature of these activities will depend on who you are.

Crafts, gardening, and similar activities are often lonely ones. A person may be in his studio, workshop, or garden day after day without talking to a soul.

People can become even more aware of the loneliness of retirement when their new activities no longer include the many daily personal contacts and exchanges they had when they were active on the job. (The case of Felix and Marge Houton presented in Chapter 5 shows how one couple resolved this problem.) The planning process outlined in this book will help you identify activities that offer the greatest degree of self-satisfaction for you.

The Important Questions

Many people feel that the special problems and planning requirements of retirement apply to others, not to them. I maintain, of course, that every person who retires can benefit from systematic planning. In case you are on the borderline and feel that the issues dealt with in this book are irrelevant to you, let me try to pique your interest by asking you a number of questions. No need to answer them right now. Just make note of the number of questions that seem to be relevant to your life.

☐ Has it occurred to you that it may be unfair to retire everyone automatically at the age of 65 or 70?

☐ Does retirement seem a little like getting fired?

☐ Did you realize that the retirement age is likely to move downward to 55, despite current legislation?

☐ Have you thought of continuing to work after you retire?

☐ Are you worried about the chances of getting a job at that age?

☐ Are you sure that the combination of social security and pension arrangements will provide you with enough money to do what you want to do in retirement?

☐ Have you stopped to consider what your life expectancy is if you are turning 65 now? (Life expectancy is about 14 years for men and longer for women.)

☐ Have you stopped to consider that even our greatest cities have inadequate facilities for the elderly?

☐ Have you noticed that today, more often than at any time in the past, children tend to live far away from their parents, especially by the time the parents retire?

☐ Did you know that a lot of people are frank to say that they can't wait to retire because they are bored and tired of being in the labor force?

☐ Are you worried about whom you will talk to and what you will do with your time when you no longer work?

☐ Are you worried that your skills may become obsolete even before you get to the age of 65? (Automation is not just affecting factory work. The computer is making radical changes in banking, marketing, and general corporate planning.)

☐ Do you assume, as many people do, that it is difficult if not impossible to reenter the labor force after reaching retirement age?

☐ Have you stopped to think that once you retire you will be able to avoid a lot of the pressure that you now carry with you from day to day?

☐ Are you fed up with commuting? Do you resent the alarm clock, look forward to retirement, and yet worry about being bored?

☐ Have you always looked upon retirement as a chance to do many things that you have never had time to do? Have you stopped lately to figure out what those things are?

☐ Have you had secret thoughts about learning new skills, perhaps through adult education, in order to undertake new activities in retirement?

☐ Have you been hesitant to talk about these vague ambitions—for example, learning to paint or taking up needlepoint (as one man I know did)—because someone might be amused?

☐ Has it occurred to you that you might shorten your workweek and actually begin some of your retirement activities, even wage-earning activities, before the normal age of retirement?

☐ Have you thought about what it will cost you to live in retirement? Are you worried that you might go broke? Would you like to plan to avoid that?

☐ Have you felt a desire to have a second career of some sort, without knowing what it would be?

If some of these questions sound familiar to you, you have reason enough to start planning for your retirement today.

Overcoming Resistance

From my own experience, and from counseling with others, I know that it is not easy to plan for retirement. If you have vague anxieties or nagging fears about what is going to happen to you, a positive antidote is to start to gather data, even if your heart is not in the effort at first. The resistance to planning is almost universal. Some people rationalize their inaction by saying that the problems will take care of themselves and they must simply be patient. You know that this approach only produces more frustration.

The average person retires with almost 20 percent of his life ahead. In terms of knowledge and perspective, you are probably at the height of your powers as a human being. It is entirely possible that some of the most rewarding and exciting experiences of your life lie ahead of you.

The point to remember is that you don't change all of a sudden just because you retire. You are the same person, with the same strong capabilities that you had before. It is simply that you are faced with a new set of circumstances. If you learn to adapt to these circumstances as you have adapted to others in the past, you will continue to lead a good life. Many people feel that their physical and mental abilities will drop off drastically just because they are going into retirement. This is not so. A large percentage of retired people continue to handle complex physical, intellectual, and creative tasks for many years after the age of 65.

Many studies confirm that the physical and mental abilities of older people are adequate to cope with and enjoy life in retirement. Newer IQ tests indicate that there is little if any impairment in intelligence. Frequently older people achieve higher scores in tests of vocabulary and word comprehension than they did when they were younger. It is generally true that their reflexes are somewhat slower and that they are more conservative. But this is compensated by their experience and ability to adjust to changing circumstances.

As an illustration: You don't drive an automobile as well as you did at 21 because you don't react to stimuli and discriminate as quickly as you used to. However, you don't have nearly as many accidents as those under 25, because you generally drive slower, do less night driving, are not tensed up after a hard day at work, and are not under as much pressure to get there in a hurry.

Studies also show that as people grow older, their behavior is inclined to differ more and more broadly from the norm. In a study of age and function by Heron and Chowns (*Age and Function,* 1967), test scores showed that variations from the norm may range from 25 percent among younger people to 60 percent in older people. This is one reason why the plans you make for retirement must be tailored to you as an individual, not to a group. Some people delude themselves into thinking that they will ignore retirement and go right on in their chosen fields. It is true that some people do continue their careers. Many doctors and some politicians remain active at their jobs long after the age of 65. But the vast majority of us cannot expect to do so.

Be honest with yourself. If it is unlikely that you can continue to practice your vocation, it is better to acknowledge it now so that you can search properly for an alternative style of life. There are no magic answers, because you are not like anyone else. But I can escort you through an interesting and well-ordered system of personal inquiry that has worked successfully for others.

The process begins with a financial analysis that will yield useful data about your own circumstances. On the basis of that, you will move into an examination of your social needs and the key questions you must answer in choosing a revised style of life. Next, you will be introduced to what I call field selection and analysis, an approach to choosing ways to spend your time in retirement. Then you will read about six specific cases that illustrate some of the most important elements of retirement planning. Finally, I will summarize the whole process for you and pass along a few words about the real meaning of affirmative retirement.

2

Financial Planning–Step by Step

AN accurate understanding of your financial prospects in retirement will influence almost all of the other key decisions that you make. For that reason, if for no other, you should direct your attention first to finances. There is another reason, however. Until you have completed your financial analysis, you may suffer from the anxiety and stress that afflict many people who are about to retire.

The Importance of Planning

In Chapter 1, I referred to the paralyzing stress that besets many people upon retirement. Anxiety, stress, and inertia are the ultimate enemies of good planning.

15

I have observed that about five years before retirement many people develop a psychological block to planning and action. It is at this time that people begin to be seriously aware of the imminence of their own retirement. Usually, they tell themselves that it is too soon to begin planning anyway, and that they will think about it later. Nevertheless, the anxiety begins to grow and eventually becomes a nagging fear. For many people, the problem is aggravated in the last few years before retirement by the feeling that they are going to be inadequate and will no longer be needed as a part of the productive workforce of society.

The effects of stress of many types have been well documented by researchers, among them Drs. Holmes and Mausde at the University of Washington. They devised a scale to rate various sources of stress that

Table 1. Stresses associated with retirement.

Adjustment to Change	Value
Fired at work (at any age)	47
Retirement	45 *
Business readjustment	39
Change in financial state	38
Change in responsibilities at work	29
Change in living conditions	25
Change in personal habits	24
Change in work hours	20
Change in residence	20
Change in recreation	19
Change in social activities	18

* Ranks tenth out of 43 stresses listed.

Source: T. H. Holmes and R. H. Rahe, "The Social Readjustment Rating Scale," *Journal of Psychosomatic Research,* Vol. 11 (1967), pp. 213–218.

arise from the need to adjust to change. The highest stress value on their scale is 100, which results from the death of a spouse. Table 1 shows the ranking of various stresses produced by retirement and other adjustments. The anxieties associated with retirement often lead to immobilization. People become confused. They feel that they cannot, by themselves, analyze all the conditions that cause their anxiety. They wish that there were a single source of difficulty so they could attack it directly. Until that anxiety begins to recede, no serious planning can occur. Fortunately, the simple process of *beginning to gather data* often causes the stress to recede sufficiently. On the other hand, if the retiree postpones action and instead tells himself that he will "get around to it soon," the anxiety begins to increase dramatically.

As long as people are immobilized by stress, they are inaccessible to help from others, even trained counselors. This is frustrating for all concerned. Planning cannot be effective until the counselor and the client recognize the problem and face it head on. People under stress often restrict themselves unnecessarily in the choice of activities and lifestyles in retirement, frequently because they fear that they will not have sufficient funds. But almost without exception, once people have clearly understood their financial picture, it is not nearly as bad as they feared. Often, they wonder why they have waited so long to clarify their financial situation.

One client seeking my advice was obviously upset about his financial prospects in retirement and had been worrying for several years. So had his wife, but they had not talked seriously about the problem until we met one evening. Then it came out into the open.

Comparing his pension with his salary, they feared they would have to change their standard of living, the first step being to sell their house and move to a less expensive area. This they dreaded doing, and it took some time for me to calm them down.

The next day this executive and I began work on financial planning. It soon became apparent that he had never before considered his real financial picture. Over the years he had been building capital through stock options and a company profit-sharing plan. In the 1960s he had also invested in growth stocks with dividend yields of about 1 percent. We did a quick estimate of his assets and potential income from deferred profit-sharing funds, social security, and elimination of the debt on exercised options. A quick review of his expenditures revealed some items that could be readily scaled down or cut without changing his standard of living.

By lunchtime we had enough data to put a financial estimate together. It was obvious that he would not have to sell his house. Elated, he telephoned his wife at their suburban home. He literally bellowed into the phone, "Jean, we don't have to sell the house! Yes, I'm sure of it. I've just spent all morning finding out that our income can be more than we thought!"

Financial analysis is a step toward decision making, and decision making is almost synonymous with planning. Successful retirement planning requires that you make a series of decisions. Those decisions start with a fundamental one: *Will I be able to maintain my present or desired standard of living in retirement?* That question cannot be answered offhand, because without knowing your financial circumstances in some detail, you cannot determine whether you will need to work or perhaps spend irreplaceable capital in order to maintain the standard of living you desire. In this and later chapters you will learn how to analyze your situation in order to make good decisions.

This chapter will lead you through a sequence of worksheets and analytical exercises for summarizing your financial condition and projecting it into retirement. The process may consume a bit of your time, but it is not, at base, a difficult one. The important thing is that you *decide right now to begin at the beginning* and to follow through to the end of the chapter.

In order to do this properly, you will need to retrieve certain records—a full year of canceled checks and credit card expenditures, for example. I will indicate the records you will need in the course of the analysis. You will find the worksheets for your financial analysis at the end of this chapter, along with samples of the first three worksheets for your guidance. The remaining worksheets depend so much on your personal situation that I have left them in outline form.

The items and amounts shown in the sample worksheets were taken from data assembled by people doing financial planning for retirement. They are given for illustrative purposes only. Feel free to add any items not shown that apply to your financial picture. Any item that does not apply to you should be ignored.

Worksheet No. 1: Assets

In Worksheet No. 1 you will summarize your assets—all things of value that you own. Some assets, like savings accounts, actually earn additional money for you. Other assets neither cost money nor earn money, but exist as a valuable resource when needed. Still other assets, like automobiles, require that you spend money in order to maintain them. Therefore, you will summarize your assets in three separate categories: assets that produce income, assets that produce neither income nor expense, and assets that require net expense.

Again, in this and in all worksheets, simply skip any line or category that does not apply to you. Your goal here is to list in manageable form what you do have and to ignore what you do not have. Later you will come back to this worksheet in order to draw conclusions about your financial needs in retirement. Let us now review the three types of assets and the information you will need for each one.

Assets Producing Income

Stocks

List each security (common or preferred), number of shares held, current dividend, cost at time of purchase, and present market value.

Bonds or Notes

List each long-term bond or note (over one year), whether government or corporate. Note the face value, current rate of interest, amount of interest, date of maturity, cost at time of purchase, and present market value.

Bank Certificates of Deposit

List each bank certificate (usually $100,000 or more) or Treasury bill (usually $10,000 or more). Note the value at time of redemption, date of redemption, cost at time of purchase, and estimated dollar and percentage rate of income.

Savings Bank Accounts

List the amount in each savings account and the rate of interest. Note the length of time money must remain in the account without penalty and the amount of penalty, if any, for early withdrawal.

Insurance Policies

List only those insurance policies that produce some income (such as dividends and annuity payments). State the face value of the policy, present cash surrender value, amount of annual dividend or annuity payment, and rate (percentage) of income relative to the total investment.

Real Estate

List all land and buildings held for profit (such as rental income). For each piece of property, note the cost of purchase, annual net income received, estimated rate of return (percentage of income against investment), and estimated current value. Do not list your own home unless you rent part of it, which would make it income producing.

Stock Options

Stock options from your company may fall into any one of the three asset categories. If you hold stock options not yet exercised, they may be income producing if the company credits you with dividends. If you have exercised the option but have not fully paid for the stock, compare the dividends with interest on your loan to determine whether they are income producing or cost you money to hold, or whether the loan and dividends are about equal.

It is not too important in which category you place stock options. Just make sure you list each one, giving the number of shares, price at which the option was granted, current market value, and length of time from granting or exercise of option to date. Estimate the rate of return, if any, on the value of your assets in the option.

Deferred Profit Sharing

Deferred profit sharing is usually paid to you in the first year of retirement, thus becoming a cash asset. If paid out in one lump sum, it is subject to capital gains tax under current regulations. If paid out in two or more installments, it is fully taxed as current income when paid.

Key Man Contracts

If you hold any key man contracts, note the annual payments over a period of years. These payments are fully taxed as current income. Technically, key man contract payments should be classified as income as received, but since the total amount will be paid out to you or your estate, you can list them here as an asset.

Other Investments

List any other forms of investment, such as holdings in oil well drilling operations or business partnerships. Follow the pattern laid out above in listing and describing the asset.

Assets Producing Neither Income Nor Expense

Paid-Up Life Insurance

Record the face value of any paid-up life insurance policy (the amount that would be paid in the event of your death). Note the cash surrender value (the money payable to you if you give up the policy), the amount that you could borrow against the policy, and the rate of interest that would be applied to that loan. For your purposes in planning for retirement, you should consider the cash surrender value of the policy as the significant figure.

Furniture and Household Goods

When you stop to think about it, you own a great many objects. These objects, taken together, are almost never worth as much as you believe they are. Nevertheless, they do have value. All furniture, household goods, and recreational equipment that do not cost money to own should be totaled here. It's also a good idea to make an inventory of the estimated real value or appraised value of certain large items, particularly silver, paintings, antiques, and other items of significant value.

Assets Requiring Net Expense

House

For a great many people approaching retirement age, the home is the largest single asset, the ownership of which calls for net expenditures. These expenses include taxes, maintenance and repair, and (if the house is not paid for) the interest portion of each mortgage payment. As we shall see later, the expenses that accrue from owning your home may figure significantly in your ability to maintain both the home and the standard of living you desire in retirement.

List the cost of the house when you acquired it, the date of purchase, the amount of mortgage paid off, and the cost of all improvements or additions you have made. Summarize as fully as you can from your checkbook records all expenditures required in owning your home (taxes, interest, maintenance, and repair).

You should also secure an estimate of the current market value of your home. There are numerous ways to do this. Many communities have real estate associations or boards that make such estimates. If your town keeps a record of sales prices for tax purposes, check recent prices for similar properties. Your banker should be familiar with the various information sources and their reliability. Also, keep in mind that a favorite topic at cocktail parties is the latest sale in the area.

Automobile

You car is another asset that costs money to maintain. Like most people, you probably will decide that a car is a necessity in retirement, just as it has always been. This is the place to calculate just what your car (or cars) costs you to own. I have seen estimates of up to $2,500 a year for automobile ownership, but I have rarely met anyone who knew just what his car was costing him.

From checkbook records or credit card records, summarize the annual cost of purchase or lease payments, gasoline and oil, maintenance, and repairs. Include the cost of depreciation, insurance, and registration. These numbers will indicate, at least approximately, what it costs you annually to own your car. Later, you may wish to do the same analysis for a less expensive car to see whether you could cut down transportation expenses. For present purposes in this summary of your assets, you are interested primarily in the present market value of your car.

Worksheet No. 2:
Summary of Assets

Worksheet No. 2 is a handy way for you to summarize the relevant information from Worksheet No. 1. The sum of your assets (all types) will appear on the bottom line of the worksheet. Once you have added together the value of all your assets, you will have done more financial analysis than most people do in their lifetimes. You already know more about your financial circumstances than most people who are approaching retirement. The information that you have supplied in building Worksheet No. 1 will be useful to you later. The analysis of your assets is now complete.

Worksheet No. 3: Pretax Income
Before and After Retirement

The next important task for you in gathering financial data is to summarize information about your income—all money or other value that you receive. As before, we will take the analysis in measured steps. Broadly speaking, there are two sources of income. One is income that derives from your assets, the other is income that derives from other sources, such as social security and pension plans.

In the first part of Worksheet No. 3 you will determine your present pretax income, contemplating no significant changes as you move into retirement. Included here will be your salary, income from savings bank accounts, and any income from securities such as stocks, bonds, notes, and Treasury bills. The second part of Worksheet No. 3 is used to estimate your after-tax income. Although your salary will be omitted, there will be a number of sources of new income. In later worksheets you will estimate your pretax income during the first year of retirement and then translate that to aftertax income. Finally, you will analyze your several sources of income in order to identify any changes that are necessary as you move into retirement.

Social Security

Social security payments can be a significant source of retirement income. The money is tax-free and can amount to over $8,000 annually for a retired couple. As you read this section, keep in mind that the formulas for calculating social security benefits are changing, and there is a considerable amount of legislation pending.

In order to understand current regulations and to assess your actual benefits, you should make a visit to your local social security office. I have always found the people in these offices to be efficient and cooperative. If you are younger than 62, find out exactly what amount you could receive between the ages of 62 and 65. Generally, it is more advantageous to wait until you are 65 to collect payments.

During your visit, check current regulations regarding the possible reduction of benefits if you receive income from work. Certainly, there will be some limit to the amount of money you can earn and still receive full social security payments. Under present regulations, workers may earn more than the stated limit if their working hours are restricted. Professionals or executives can work 15 hours a month, no matter how much money they receive for that work, without any reduction in social security payments. Some nonprofessionals can work up to 45 hours a month without loss of benefits. In the future, if you consider the possibility of undertaking part-time work, you will have to know precisely what the then-current regulations provide.

Currently, the law allows you to work as much as you choose with no limit on earnings after you reach the age of 72. There is considerable public interest in having the age limit reduced, along with other reforms. For example, some people think that it is not fair to have to pay social security *taxes* on all income from work as long as you live, even if you work until you are 100 years old. Others feel that working after 65 should increase social security benefits when you do, in fact, retire.

When you have done this research, list on Worksheet No. 3 the social security payments you will receive during your first year of retirement.

Pension

The organization you work for can tell you exactly how much money your pension fund will pay you in the first year of retirement. Find out also what the formula has been for increasing pension payments. You may be able to project that payments will be increased again during your retirement.

Other Sources of Income

You will have to make a temporary and perhaps arbitrary decision about your expected income from deferred profit sharing if you participate in such a plan. Also, at the point at which you collect this lump sum of money, there will be a startling capital gains tax, which could run as high as 40 percent. You will have to calculate the net benefit from deferred profit sharing and make a plan for investing it over a period of time. Once you have such a plan, enter the benefit for the first year of your retirement in the appropriate section of the worksheet.

If you have any annuity payments which are payable upon retirement, they should be listed as future income.

Stock options are often considered a good way of saving before retirement, since it is hoped they will appreciate in value (which is tax-free until the stock is sold and the gain realized). There is usually a time limit within which the option must be exercised. You will probably find that on retirement it pays to exercise any outstanding stock options and sell enough to liquidate debts incurred in exercising the option.

Finally, think carefully about any other real sources of income (other than your assets) that will accrue to you in retirement and list those in the appropriate space.

Income from Assets

If you look back at Worksheet No. 1, you will find a list of assets that will produce income for you. For all those assets that you expect to retain rather than sell, calculate the annual income during your first year of retirement. List the amounts on Worksheet No. 3.

Now, add up all the income you expect to receive during your first year of retirement and place the figure for *total pretax income* on the bottom line.

As a rule of thumb, economists estimate that you will be able to maintain your present standard of living if your aftertax income is about 75 percent of your preretirement income after taxes. Since you will have a lower income, be in a lower tax bracket, and have double personal exemptions, you will pay a lower income tax. In addition, income from social security is tax-free.

Normally there will be a reduction in expenses because you are no longer working. For example, you will no longer have the expense of commuting and will probably be able to get along with one car less. In addition, you will need less clothing and of a different type. One retired president of a large corporation told me he hadn't purchased a suit in ten years.

Worksheet No. 4: Aftertax Income in Retirement

I advise you to estimate your *probable after tax income* in retirement by using substantially the same deductions you have used in recent years. You can use last year's tax return as a guide if you had no unusual or nonrecurring items that year. A safer method is to use an average of the last three years to calculate your taxable income and your rate of taxation. Remember that personal exemptions on federal income double after the age of 65. Tax law is always under revision, so it is important to be sure that you have the most recent regulations in hand. You can use current tax tables as a general index to your aftertax income.

If your tax situation is complicated, you may find it helpful to obtain the services of a tax consultant, either from an independent accounting firm or from a bank. Sometimes, it is difficult to figure out just how much your tax burden will be reduced when you reach 65. One executive was subject to substantial capital gains tax upon retirement. He was advised to change his residence from Connecticut to Florida immediately, because Connecticut imposes at least a 3 percent capital gains tax, while Florida imposes none. Because he owned a house in Connecticut and a condominium in Florida, the only requirement was that he spend six months out of Connecticut.

Once again, keep in mind that tax laws keep changing, so specific cases are cited here only with reluctance. This worksheet will help you organize your information and then reduce your total to reflect approximately what your aftertax income will be in your first year of retirement.

Worksheet No. 5: Preretirement Expenditures

We now shift from questions of assets and income to a consideration of your past, present, and future expenditures.

Attitudes Toward Capital

For almost everyone, the age of retirement signals that the highest earning years have passed. You can no longer count on continued savings programs to augment your capital assets or to replace any capital that you may use or lose. This intensifies your need for a sound and well-planned program for conserving and/or using existing capital. In approaching this problem, you should think carefully about all the ways, sometimes disguised ways, in which you have been saving over the years.

Besides bank accounts, there have been life insurance payments, amortization of your mortgage, contributions to deferred profit sharing, and perhaps company stock purchase plans. You should examine the stocks, bonds, and other investment items in your portfolio to assess the security of the capital invested there. You should also analyze your expected return on investment from these properties during retirement—income either from dividends or from possible capital gains.

You will have to decide whether to liquidate certain holdings or keep them as a source of benefit to you in retirement. If you are not able to do this alone, I urge you to obtain the advice of an investment counselor before proceeding in any direction.

One retired executive I know had been very busy and successful in his working life. Besides accumulating stock in his own company, he had bought substantial growth stocks. But he met with indifferent success, mainly because he had been too preoccupied with his job to pay much attention to his investments. After going to his local bank for advice, he decided to keep his company stock, which had excellent growth and income possibilities. This plus his pension put him in a high tax bracket, so he decided to sell his other stocks and buy tax-exempt bonds. Then he had the bank set up a trust fund for his income. Thus he was relieved of all financial worries and was able to lead an active retirement, unfettered by day-to-day monetary concerns.

As you will see later in the chapter, you will have to exercise fine judgment in deciding what amount of accumulated capital (if any) you wish to spend in retirement and what amount you wish to retain for its continued income and growth. In the end, it will come down to deciding whether, in terms of your intended lifestyle, you will need a greater or smaller proportion of your capital as income.

Calculating Preretirement Expenditures

All the information you need about your preretirement expenditures can be summarized in Worksheet No. 5. You will need your check stubs and bank statements for the last twelve months. You may also need to refer to recent IRS reports. If you have been careful in the expenditure of money, chances are good that you will have some kind of budget to refer to as well.

For the moment, your task is one of research and recording. Do not concern yourself with prognostications about the future. That will be the substance of Worksheet No. 6. In filling out Worksheet No. 5, you probably will find it necessary to generate some expenditure figures on separate worksheets, then record the annual totals in the spaces indicated.

Remember that some portion of your monthly and annual expenditures has been made in cash. You will have to be particularly attentive in allocating the expenditure of pocket money. A good way to do this is to follow yourself mentally through a typical workday or workweek, and then record all those occasions on which you paid for things in cash. Also, pay particular attention to recording any large or unusual expenditures that are not a repetitive part of your spending pattern. It is important that you stay with this exercise until you have exhausted your resources, your records, and your memory in accounting for the largest possible portion of your expenditures during the past twelve months. If the exercise is to be maximally useful to you, you must use the miscellaneous and incidental category only sparingly and reluctantly. Try to identify your expenses as specifically as possible.

Analyzing Past Expenditures

Study Worksheet No. 5 carefully to determine all the important ways in which your spending habits will change as you enter retirement. It is helpful to look at four major types of expenses to see whether they will continue as in the past or change without affecting your standard of living significantly.

1. Examine large discretionary expenses such as extended trips, new furniture, home remodeling, club dues, and entertainment. Will these items change in the future? In retirement, it is entirely possible that your discretionary spending will take on a new pattern. For example, if your house has recently been painted, you could probably sell it, if you wanted to, without further painting expense.

2. Identify clearly those expenses that are nonrecurring. It is safe to eliminate these items from your analysis of expenditures in retirement.

3. Look carefully at all those expenditures that arise out of a working lifestyle—commutation tickets and other transportation costs, clothing, business luncheons, entertainment, and so on. Again, follow yourself mentally through a typical workday or workweek and isolate those expenditures that will not be necessary in retirement.

4. Study all your assets that require net expense. The largest of these will probably be your home. As I explained elsewhere in this book, the complex decisions that surround the choice of housing may depend on much more than financial considerations. Nevertheless, for purposes of this analysis, you should concentrate heavily at this time on the *financial* aspects of housing.

If you own your home, figure out precisely what it

is costing you, so that later you can compare the cost with alternative solutions to the housing problem. Real estate agents can give you a fairly good estimate of the present value of your house and will be only too pleased to show you houses for sale. Also, while you are investigating housing alternatives, you should consider buying a condominium or renting a house or apartment. You will want to calculate the net difference in a number of ways.

I remember one couple who lived alone in a large house that required considerable expense for upkeep. They decided to sell the house when they retired. It brought $80,000. They bought a much smaller, but adequate house in the same area for $55,000. (Both figures are net of brokerage fees, moving expenses, and the incidentals involved in changing residences.) The move freed up approximately $25,000 in capital before taxes. Reasonably invested, that money provided about $1,500 annually in additional income. Furthermore, their new taxes were $880 less. After capital gains taxes, which usually are reduced for people over 65, my friends ended up with a net gain of about $2,000 per year without sacrificing their living standards.

Another large asset requiring net expense is your automobile. American families generally consider a car to be a necessity of life. As noted earlier, automobile costs can run as high as $2,500 a year. The expense becomes even more burdensome if you have a second car. Stop and ask yourself whether you will need the second car after you retire. What precisely do you use the second car for during a working week? If you were not working, could you do without that car? If you would need the second car only infrequently in retirement—or the first car, for that matter—maybe you should consider renting a car whenever you need one. Some people have found that it is considerably cheaper to rent an automobile for specific occasions than to own one. My purpose here is not to pressure you into giving up your automobiles, but rather to encourage you to get the facts about what a car is costing you.

Worksheet No. 6: Probable Expenditures During the First Year of Retirement

Worksheet No. 6 is exactly like Worksheet No. 5, except that you are now going to fill it out to reflect your intended lifestyle and expenditures *during retirement*. This is an imprecise exercise, but it is well worth doing at this stage of your planning.

You and I both know that before you derive a fully satisfactory solution to the financial and social aspects of retirement, you will change your plans a number of times. Worksheet No. 6 will serve as a first effort, subject to modification. You will no doubt find, as many people have, that a number of really important questions have to be answered before you can project retirement expenditures. These questions relate not only to financial considerations but also to the use of your time and the lifestyle you will follow when you leave your job.

One problem that frequently arises is deciding where to live. Some people prefer city life, with all its cultural benefits. Others move to the Sun Belt for its relaxed atmosphere and pleasant climate. One man I know worked as a researcher in New York. Both he and his wife loved the city. Unfortunately, she developed a respiratory problem, and the doctors decided that she should live in a warmer and drier climate. After retirement they moved to Southern California, which was ideal. In their new location there were research facilities for him and the proper climate for her. The opportunities are many and varied.

In analyzing your retirement expenses, you will find it helpful to refer frequently to the summary that you have prepared in Worksheet No. 5. Naturally, you will not be able to identify all the minor departures from past history, but it is important to identify the large ones that will have a significant impact on your financial circumstances.

Worksheet No. 7: Comparison of Aftertax Income with Projected Expenditures in Retirement

Worksheet No. 7 requires no new research, only a simple calculation. Almost certainly, it is a calculation you have already made in your head as you prepared Worksheet No. 4 and Worksheet No. 6. Here, you are going to find out whether your first approximations of income and expenditures in retirement are compatible with your intended lifestyle. On this sheet subtract your *total annual expenditures* as shown in Worksheet No. 6 from your *total aftertax income* as shown in Worksheet No. 4. If you find a deficit, don't become concerned. In the next section I will show you techniques for dealing with that deficit.

Spending Irreplaceable Capital

To say that the subject of spending irreplaceable capital is highly charged with emotion is an understatement. Don't forget that all your calculations so far have been based on preserving your existing capital assets, primarily in the form of savings and investments. Many people assume automatically that they must move through retirement without reducing their existing capital assets. Whenever I advise people to consider a gradual liquidation of assets in order to produce additional retirement income, I encounter three kinds of reactions:

1. "I was brought up never to touch my capital." This sentiment, based on the Puritan ethic, is deeply embedded in our culture and, in fact, in many cultures around the world.

2. "I had an uncle who spent his capital in retirement, and he ended up on relief." Many people fear going broke if they begin to spend capital assets.

3. "I plan to leave all my money to the kids." Many people take it for granted that they will leave an inheritance. All too often, I have seen people with significant capital assets cramp their retirement lifestyle seriously in order to preserve some sacred inheritance. While I know that this is a natural and generous instinct, I often point out that their children may well be 50 years old before they inherit any money from their parents and, in fact, may not need the money at all. Most people never consider that their children may prefer to have their parents live better during retirement, especially if it frees the children from having to make difficult contributions to the parents' welfare.

A Formula for the Gradual Expenditure of Capital

The formula I recommend for the gradual expenditure of capital should be used only as a frame of reference. Ultimately, you will have to devise your own formula to meet your needs and wishes. The purpose of the formula I recommend is to increase your cash flow during retirement sufficiently to allow you to pursue the lifestyle that will make you happy. Furthermore, if you use the formula, or some modification of it, your income will be fairly steady during retirement and you will never go broke. Keep in mind also that the formula can be modified during your retirement whenever you see fit and that it in no way restricts your freedom in deciding what part of your accumulated capital to preserve for inheritance purposes.

The formula is based on the premise that a man or his wife may live to be 90 years old. Now, statistically, the odds are that you will not live much beyond 80. I use the age of 90 to provide a cushion. If you follow the guidelines precisely, and if you do reach the age of 90, you will still have some of your capital remaining. Here is the formula:

The percentage of capital that may be spent starts at 5 percent per year, at the age of 65, and increases by 1 percent every five years.

All percentages are calculated on the basis of remaining capital at the end of each year, not the original total. This has the effect of maintaining a relatively stable income or cash flow from the combination of capital usage (liquidation) and income from remaining capital invested. Perhaps the easiest way to understand this is to look at the figures in Table 2.

Figure 1 diagrams the effect of the formula on each $1,000 of capital between the ages of 65 and 90. The lower portion represents the capital that is to be withheld.

As you can see in the column at the right of Table 2, the combination of annual withdrawal (or liquida-

Table 2. Gradual use of each $1,000 of capital, from age 65 to age 90.

Age	Remaining Capital, Beginning of Year	Annual Withdrawal of Remaining Capital *		Income from Remaining Capital †	Usable Cash Available
		Percent	Amount		
65	$1,000.00	5	$50.00	$60.00	$110.00
69	814.26	5	40.71	48.85	89.57
70	773.55	6	46.41	46.41	92.83
74	603.96	6	36.24	36.24	72.47
75	567.72	7	39.74	34.06	73.80
79	424.68	7	29.73	25.48	55.21
80	394.95	8	31.60	23.70	55.30
84	282.94	8	22.64	16.98	39.62
85	270.30	9	24.33	16.22	40.55
89	185.36	9	16.68	11.12	27.80
90	168.68	10	16.87	10.12	26.99

* Annual withdrawal is not taxed unless there is capital gain or loss. If a capital loss exists, there will actually be a reduction in your taxes. Withdrawals need not be adhered to rigidly. They may be a little more one year, a little less another.

† Income from capital is arbitrarily set at 6 percent.

tion) of existing capital plus income from investment of remaining capital yields a total increment to income that declines over the years. Up until age 80, the combination of income and capital withdrawn under the formula will be greater than the income from the original capital alone. At age 90, when cash flow has been reduced, you still will have income from social security and pension benefits. Naturally, if this formula yields insufficient additional income (see Worksheet No. 7), you will have to consider modifying your lifestyle during retirement. This may take the form of reduced ambitions with regard to housing and enter-

Figure 1. Gradual reduction of capital.

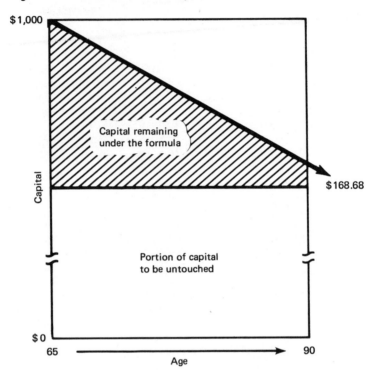

tainment, or it may involve some part-time work. These topics will be pursued in later chapters.

As noted earlier, this formula for the gradual expenditure of income is not sacred or final. You have total discretion over the rules by which it is applied. The most important thing to decide at this point is how much of your accumulated capital is expendable under the formula. Most people prefer to reserve a part of their capital for inheritance purposes. If this is the case, you should exclude that sum from the beginning. You can then anticipate a larger capital reserve at age 90, either for your use or for inheritance. Circumstances may dictate that you do not have to consider your investment in your home to be expendable, especially in the beginning. These decisions are highly personal ones and cannot be dictated by any counselor. The exercise that you have to go through involves a careful counterbalancing of your retirement goals, your inheritance goals, and your financial prospects for retirement.

Tax Benefits of Retirement

We have presupposed in this analysis that all calculations ultimately must be converted to aftertax figures. This may not be as simple as it appears. Many of the rules of taxation and exemption will change as you enter your sixty-fifth year. You should check to make sure that you have taken all tax advantages into account. Look at your previous tax records covering the last few years. Make out a new pro forma income tax based on the changes you know about and the changes you can research from the tax law.

Under present rules, for example, you and your wife will be allowed four standard deductions instead of two.

Also, since your direct income from your pension will be lower than your working salary, you will be in a lower tax bracket. Your social security benefits will be tax-free, as will any existing capital you use. Any assets you sell will be subject to capital gains tax or credit for the amount of your capital gain or loss. Usually there are losses to counterbalance gains, at least for the first few years.

In converting to an aftertax basis under new rules of taxation and exemption, you may want to secure the help of a tax expert. It should be clear to you by now that the important decisions you make about retirement should be based on the most precise projections you can derive.

Now that you have filled out all the worksheets, you should be reasonably familiar with your financial prospects for retirement. Your analysis will form the basis for a number of decisions affecting your happiness and fulfillment during your retirement years. Throughout this book, you will find it useful to refer frequently to these worksheets. For example, as you develop new hypotheses about the use of your time during retirement, you may find it necessary to revise these tables in order to reflect your new designs. I know that some of you will alter your intentions radically as a result of the systematic planning that is recommended in the following chapters. You may want to make a new set of worksheets, based on those shown at the end of this chapter, to accommodate major changes in your thinking. Be flexible. Don't hesitate to undertake the entire analysis again if you revise your goals.

After going through the financial planning exercise, you may have a number of additional questions—on wills, trusts, and so on. These issues are not initiated by retirement and so are not dealt with in this book. There are numerous sources of authoritative information available.

Now let us sum up the results of your labors. First and foremost, you should have some idea of whether you can maintain your present standard of living in retirement. If you cannot, you should now know how much supplemental earnings you will need (or the extent to which you must curtail expenses). You also have a pretty good idea of your assets and income in retirement. This information will assist you in investment planning, either on your own or with an investment counselor.

SAMPLE WORKSHEET NO. 1
ASSETS

Assets Producing Income

Stocks		*Current Value*
300 shares	American Home Products at 33 Purchased 5/5/75 at 36¾—$11,025. Loss (long-term) $1,125. Dividend $1. Return on investment 3%	$ 9,900
300 shares	American Home Products at 33 Purchased 1/7/75 at 33⅛—$9,375. Loss $375. Dividend $1. Return on investment 3%.	9,900
500 shares	American Telephone & Telegraph at 57 Bought 12/7/73 at 46⅞—$23,450. Gain $5,050. Dividend $3.80. Return on investment 8%.	28,500
200 shares	General Motors at 68½ Purchased 1/15/75 at 58½—$11,720. Gain $1,980. Dividend $2.40. Return on investment 4%.	13,700
200 shares	Chase REIT at 3¼ Purchased 5/18/71 at 47⅝—$9,525. Loss $8,875. Dividend ——. Return on investment ——.	650

Bonds or Notes		
$10,000	Ford Notes at 100 Purchased at 100. Gain/loss ____. Interest 8⅜. Return on investment 8⅜%. Due to be redeemed 11/76.	10,000

Certificates of Deposit or U.S. Treasury Bills		
$10,000	U.S. Treasury bills Purchased 11/18/75 at 97½. Gain/loss ____. Return on investment $250 (5%). Due to be redeemed 5/14/76 at 100.	10,000

Savings Bank Accounts		
$5,000	XYZ Savings Bank Can withdraw any quarter. Interest (return on investment) 5½%.	5,000
$2,000	RYL Commercial Bank Interest (day of deposit to day of withdrawal) 4½%.	2,000

Insurance Policies		
$10,000	Life insurance policy annuity cash surrender value Payments after 65—$650 per year. Nominal ROI 6½%. Actual income considering loss of capital is negative.	7,600

		Current Value
Stock Options		
1,000 shares	Stock options, General RK Corp. at $30 Must be exercised on retirement. Stock currently at $50. From that point on consider as cash or income-producing investment, depending on whether all or part is sold.	20,000
Deferred Profit Sharing		
$30,000	Deferred profit-sharing plan Paid in one sum on retirement—must then be reinvested in income producing securities. Since subject to capital gains tax, it would be conservative to assess net value of approximately 77%.	23,000
	Total assets producing income	$140,250

Assets Producing Neither Income Nor Expense

		Current Value
Paid-up Life Insurance		
$20,000	20-payment life insurance policy (paid-up) Cash surrender value $16,200. Might be invested in income-producing assets.	$ 16,200
Furniture and Household Goods		
$10,000	Furniture, household goods, antiques, works of art It is usually good to get an appraisal of resale value.	10,000
	Total assets producing neither income nor expense	26,200

Assets Requiring Net Expense

Own Home	Own home—net estimated value Bought 4/6/75. Cost with improvements $32,000. Estimated sale value $80,000. Mortgage $20,000. Interest 6½%—$1,300. Taxes $2,700. Maintenance and repairs $1,200. Total expense $5,200. Capital gain if sold $28,000. (Note: if over 65, IRS allows up to $20,000 rebate on capital gains tax.)	$ 60,000
Automobile	1975 Chevrolet appraised 1966 Volkswagen appraised (I leave it to you to figure out what each car costs in depreciation, insurance, repairs, maintenance. I estimate that my car costs $2,000 annually.)	4,200 225
	Total assets requiring net expense	$ 64,425

SAMPLE WORKSHEET NO. 2
SUMMARY OF ASSETS

Assets producing income	$140,250
Assets producing neither income nor expense	26,200
Assets requiring net expense	64,425
Total assets	$230,875

SAMPLE WORKSHEET NO. 3
PRETAX INCOME BEFORE AND AFTER RETIREMENT

Pretax Income Before Retirement		*Annual Amount*
Salary		$25,000
Stocks—Annual Income		
600 shares American Home	600	
500 shares AT&T	1,900	
200 shares GM	480	
	2,980	2,980
Other—Annual Income		
$10,000 Ford Notes	837	
$10,000 Treasury Bills	500	
$ 5,000 XYZ Savings Bank	275	
$ 2,000 RYL Savings Bank	90	
	1,702	1,702
	Annual Total	$29,682

Pretax Income After Retirement	
Social Security *	$ 5,000
Pension (40% of salary) *	10,000
Other Sources *	
Annuity—life insurance	650
$20,000 in stock options (estimate 5% income)	1,000
$30,000 in deferred profit sharing (estimate 5% income)	1,500
Income from Assets	
Stocks (as shown above)	2,980
Other (as shown above)	1,702
Annual total †	$22,832

* New income after retirement = $18,150.
† Total income after retirement = 77% of preretirement income.
Rule of thumb: about 75% needed to maintain living standard.

WORKSHEET NO. 1
ASSETS

Assets Producing Income

Stocks   *Current Value*

Total $

Bonds or Notes

Total $

Bank Certificates of Deposit

Total $

Savings Bank Accounts

Total $

Insurance Policies

Total $

Real Estate

Total $

Stock Options

Total $

Deferred Profit Sharing

Total $

Key Man Contracts   *Current Value*

Total $

Other

Total $

Total Assets Producing Income $ _____

Assets Producing Neither Income nor Expense
Paid-up Life Insurance   *Current Value*

Total $

Furniture and Household Goods

Total $

Total assets producing neither
income nor expense $ _____

Assets Requiring Net Expense
Own Home

Total $

Automobile

Total $

Other

Total $

Total assets requiring net expense $ _____

WORKSHEET NO. 2
SUMMARY OF ASSETS

Assets producing income $ _____
Assets producing neither income nor
  expense $ _____
Assets requiring net expense $ _____

  Total assets $ _____

WORKSHEET NO. 3
PRETAX INCOME BEFORE AND AFTER RETIREMENT

                                                    Annual
Pretax Income Before Retirement   *Amount*
Salary $ _____
Stocks—Annual Income   _____   _____

Other—Annual Income   _____   _____

                           Annual total $ _____

Pretax Income After Retirement

Social security *
Pension (% of Salary) *
Other Sources *
  Annuity—Life Insurance
  $,000 in stock options (estimate 5% income)
  $,000 in deferred profit sharing (estimate 5% income)
Income from Assets
  Stocks (as shown above, if not sold)
  Other notes (as shown above, if not sold)
                           Annual total † $ _____

* New income after retirement = $ _____ .
† Total income after retirement = —% of preretirement income.
Rule of thumb: about 75% needed to maintain living standard.

WORKSHEET NO. 4
AFTERTAX INCOME IN RETIREMENT

1. Pretax income, first year of retirement $ _____
2. Average deductions, last three years _____
3. Personal exemptions in retirement _____
4. Sum of lines 2 and 3 $ _____
5. Line 1 minus line 4, or taxable income $ _____
6. Rate of taxation, first year of retirement _____
7. Line 5 times rate in line 6 $ _____
8. Line 5 minus line 6, or projected aftertax income $ _____

WORKSHEET NO. 5
PRERETIREMENT EXPENDITURES

Amount

Real estate taxes and mortgage interest
House insurance: fire, theft, liability
Rent
Medical: doctor, dentist, hospital, drugs
Credit card: meals, entertainment, clothes
Liquor
Light, heat, fuel oil, telephone
Books, magazines, newspapers
Contributions
Laundry and cleaning
Home maintenance: plumber, gardener, etc.
Clothing
Club dues and expenses: activities, meals, etc.
Maid service
Vacation
Food: supermarket, restaurants
Car: gas, license, repairs, tires, insurance, etc.
Commutation
Household supplies
Presents
Miscellaneous—cash not allocated
   (should be less than 10% of total)
Federal income tax
State income tax
Local income tax
Other

Total $ _____

WORKSHEET NO. 6
PROBABLE EXPENDITURES
DURING THE FIRST YEAR OF RETIREMENT

Amount

Real estate taxes and mortgage interest
House insurance: fire, theft, liability
Rent
Medical: doctor, dentist, hospital, drugs
Credit card: meals, entertainment, clothes
Liquor
Light, heat, fuel oil, telephone
Books, magazines, newspapers
Contributions
Laundry and cleaning
Home maintenance: plumber,
    gardener, etc.
Clothing
Club dues and expenses: activities, meals, etc.
Maid service
Vacation
Food: supermarket, restaurants
Car: gas, license, repairs, tires, insurance, etc.
Commutation
Household supplies
Presents
Miscellaneous—cash not allocated
    (should be less than 10% of total)
Federal income tax
State income tax
Local income tax
Other

Total $ _____

WORKSHEET NO. 7
COMPARISON OF AFTERTAX INCOME
WITH PROJECTED EXPENDITURES IN
RETIREMENT

1. Aftertax income, first year of retirement $ _____

2. Projected expenses, first year of
   retirement   _____

3. Line 1 minus line 2, or
   projected excess (deficit) $ _____

3

Choices in Your Style of Living

ARMED with some useful facts about your present and future financial circumstances, you can now examine some of the choices that retirement presents. There are decisions to be made about the lifestyle you intend to pursue in retirement. Even if your means are limited, you have a number of options, and you will find that there are ways of making the most of what you have. In fact, this kind of careful planning is especially important if your means are going to be somewhat restricted.

Your task in this chapter is twofold. First, you must clarify your needs and wants. Second, you must evaluate these needs and wants against your expected financial realities so you can make the choices that will lead to a satisfying lifestyle.

I like to think of retirement as a shift from a goal-oriented existence to a reflective one, a period when you can carefully consider the quality of your life. Society has defined a structure for your life until the time of retirement. At each stage you have a set of tasks to perform, such as getting an education, getting a job, getting married, raising a family, and acquiring skills in order to move up in your job. When you retire, you are free to do as you please with your financial and mental resources.

Retirement is such a new phenomenon that society has not yet set up standards or norms to cover it. Financial-help and community activities are springing up all about us, but many of these services are so scattered that retired people do not know about them. Therefore, despite all the assistance available, the decision of how to live a satisfactory life remains primarily with you.

In looking ahead to retirement, people follow two general patterns. Some think primarily in terms of pursuing certain valued *activities*—professional and vocational, educational, or leisure. Others think first of the need for *social integration*—a sense of belonging, of being wanted and respected.

Naturally, everyone must think in terms of both activities and social integration in order to arrange a satisfactory retirement. Each person, however, must have a starting point for analysis. In this chapter, we will concentrate on questions pertaining to social lifestyle. In the next chapter we will examine a system for planning activities and structuring the use of your time. According to your style, you may pursue your planning with either one as a primary consideration.

The Need for Social Integration

Whether retired or not, no one likes to be isolated from other people. We are happy when we are rooted in regular personal contacts and friendships. We need to occupy a regular place in the lives of others—in the family, in business, and in social institutions. Well over half of the people I have counseled have mentioned social integration as their most profound apprehension in approaching retirement. They don't express it in those terms. Primarily, it comes out in the blunt statement, "I am lonesome."

When an executive retires, he leaves a business institution, but he also leaves the company of other people—people with whom he has spent much time, people to whom he has felt connected in a common enterprise. His position in the community declines. There is a real need to rebuild a position of acceptance.

One has only to look at the vast and growing number of "retirement colonies" across the country that accept or are designed solely for retired people to realize the need for social integration. These groups are self-contained communities and can run from the shuffleboard-type colony to the expensive development built around a golf course. All of them have a community center or recreation hall and frequently a large communal swimming pool. The life of the inhabitants centers on group activities such as bingo games, poker, and bridge. A main event is the "happy hour," when people meet for cocktails. This ritual serves to introduce new residents and start their social integration into the community.

It has been my experience over years of counseling

that loneliness—the need for social integration—is a more vital problem than financial security in retirement. This is especially true of people in middle and upper-middle income groups. On a trip to Florida recently I looked up a retired couple who had sold their home in a Philadelphia suburb and bought a condominium near Sarasota. They told me that the first year was difficult. They had trouble meeting people, people whom they liked and who shared their interests—playing cards, going fishing, playing golf, and making small expeditions. However, after that original period of adjustment they became so busy socially that they had to be selective about the invitations they accepted. They even became a bit disillusioned about their old home town. Most of the people there had moved away or died. The people moving into Sarasota were younger or more vigorous, and my friends were much too busy to worry about older retired people.

Later, we will discuss the implications of moving. Here let me say simply that the relocation that may accompany retirement will sever still more personal ties. In planning your retirement lifestyle, do not make the mistake of overlooking the need for social integration. I believe that it is not necessary for anyone to be lonely in retirement. Lack of understanding and inadequate coping with the problem are the major causes of loneliness.

Since this book is designed to be comprehensive and to assist you in intelligent planning, it is perhaps appropriate to look at some of the major causes of the decline of social integration in our culture. For many people, these environmental influences become salient for the first time at the point of retirement, but the decline in social integration is a more general phenomenon in our society, affecting virtually everyone at all stages of life.

The first major cause of the decline in social integration is the accelerated trend toward *urbanization.* This trend probably started even before your parents' time. Ever since the end of westward expansion, Americans have been moving from the farms to the cities, and then to the suburbs. Many have observed that it is much harder to feel a sense of belonging, of being part of a community, in a large city. Older generations were not isolated. In rural communities everybody knew practically everyone else. Farming gave people common interests and common ground for conversation and sharing. Institutions were few. Life centered around the church, the grange, and various fraternal organizations like the Masons, Knights of Columbus, Elks, and Odd Fellows.

In contrast, apartment dwellers in today's cities barely nod to one another when they meet in the elevator. There is precious little common ground for discussing daily events when one tenant is an advertising executive, another is a policeman, and others up and down the hall are garment workers or food distributors. For all its technological advances, the city does not offer many satisfying activities for the elderly. Unlike the farm, there aren't any chores to occupy them and make them feel useful. The unfortunate result is that older citizens become a burden on others.

This leads to the second major cause of the decline in social integration: the decline in effectiveness of the family, both nuclear and extended. The time when cousins, aunts, nephews, and grandparents were in continuous contact has virtually disappeared. Most of us have to think back many years to remember when ten to twenty members of our family gathered for occasional meals or celebrations. The cohesiveness of the nuclear family has also declined materially. Parents and children lead practically separate lives from the time the children reach puberty. People are tied more closely to outside institutions than to the home. Divorce breaks up about one-third of all families.

The problem of isolation affects suburban areas as well as large urban centers. To a certain extent suburban communities fare slightly better: kids in the neighborhood tend to bring parents together socially during the school years; residents share a number of concerns, such as PTA meetings, zoning, garbage collection, and bond issues; clubs for tennis, golf, and swimming provide gathering places where people can feel a part of things. But there are limitations.

One retiring executive in Fairfield County, Connecticut, described the situation well. He said that his town was a bedroom community for working commuters going to New York City. "There is no one around during weekday working hours. Everyone is active and aggressive in his work, and unless you are a part of it, you get left out completely. Friendships are transitory, because people are always moving in and out. What social life there is revolves around the cocktail party, the country club, and bridge." I should point out that everyone is not as well provided for as this man. At least he had enough money to maintain membership in clubs where he could relate to other people regularly.

A third reason for the decline in social integration is the increasing mobility of American families. Americans are continually moving from one place to another. The net result is that any one family may not have ten close relatives within 1,000 miles of where they live. The scattering continues. By the time you reach 65, it is likely that a great many members of your family will be far removed from where you live.

Look around your own community and try to think of people who are native to the area. People are always moving for a better job, a better climate, or perhaps, more simply, a better cultural environment. We scatter ourselves in the interest of advancement. When I retired, my family was spread from Vermont to California. In many parts of the country today, it isn't uncommon for a couple to drive 50 miles for dinner or entertainment. Even for these casual pleasures we take one more step away from community life.

It is not only families that scatter. Friends begin to retire and move away. Unfortunately, the death of friends begins to be an issue. One very socially active family in our neighborhood had six couples, all close friends, move away in a short period, as did all the couples' children. They were hard put to assemble a group of old friends for Thanksgiving dinner.

If you reach retirement age in a community that is satisfactory to you and in which you are as close as you want to be to other members of your family, you are among the fortunate few. You are among a still more select minority if that community offers the kinds of activities that you hope to pursue during your retirement years. You are especially fortunate if you have all these things *and* the financial circumstances that will allow you the luxury of remaining where you are. In order to achieve social integration and a proper mix of satisfying activities, a great many retirees decide that relocation is part of the answer.

Where Will You Live in Retirement?

There are four main reasons why people choose to move soon after retirement. In every case, the reason is related to their wish to pursue the best possible lifestyle in their new circumstances. Your own plans may or may not include a move, but most people cannot make the decision without considering the following factors.

The first and most obvious reason for relocating is financial. At a purely practical level, you may be unable to maintain your present dwelling and still have enough money for the other things you want to do with your new freedom. Because you have already done your financial summary, you know that owning a home, for example, constitutes a very large overhead.

Even if you are located in a community that satisfies your other needs, you may find it advantageous to move to a smaller house or to an apartment. Perhaps property values in the community are very high. During the working years many people move to affluent suburbs in order to be close to work in the city and to have good schools and social advantages for their children. Ask yourself whether your present location retains the advantages it originally had. In any case, is your house too large for your present needs?

For the sake of example, let us assume that your present house is worth $50,000 on today's market. Let us assume further that your house is paid for, or almost paid for. You may conclude that, therefore, it isn't costing you very much to live there. This is not so, because the capital you have tied up in that house might earn you $4,000 a year if it were invested in something else, such as high-grade (8 percent) bonds. If your taxes are $1,000 and you spend an additional $1,000 annually for maintenance and repairs, the annual cost of owning your house is about $6,000.

If you chose to sell your house, you would have several options. You could probably move to an apartment and live there for much less money. If it is important to you to own your own place, you might consider buying a condominium or a smaller house in a less expensive neighborhood. Even with the new investment or rental payment, you might well have enough money left over to travel or pursue other forms of recreation that you have deferred for too long.

One of my clients thought he was going to have to take a part-time job in retirement in order to make ends meet. As it turned out, he was assuming blindly that he had to maintain the dwelling he had lived in for 25 years. He sold his house and moved into a retirement condominium 400 miles away, near his daughter's family, and was able to take a cruise every year with the money he saved. He did not have to have a job. Furthermore, he felt relieved not to have the responsibility of maintaining a house and yard.

Recreation itself may be a sufficient reason to consider a move. An avid fisherman may welcome having a lake or the ocean near his door. Some people have combined recreation and living in their solution to the housing problem. For example, a manufacturer of mobile homes runs annual tours to all parts of the world. There may be as many as 500 trailers on a pre-planned tour, which can last for several months. Trailer owners travel in a caravan and enjoy a great sense of community. I have run into these caravans in South Africa and in Mexico. The people come from all states, and almost all of them are retired. One woman said to me, "This sure beats sitting on the porch, rocking in Muncie, Indiana." If you are active and in good health, you may wish to break new ground by taking up forms of recreation that you have never tried before.

Many people choose to relocate in retirement because they seek a drier or warmer climate. Florida, Texas, New Mexico, Arizona, Southern California—the so-called Sun Belt—all have significant populations of retired people who have moved there from harsher climates. Some have moved purely out of preference; others move for reasons of health.

Another reason retirees move is to be near old friends and family. This can be especially important for people who have gone through a number of company moves, rarely living in one community more than five or six years—an average tenure in the suburbs of many large cities. If you are living in suburban Chicago, Seattle, or Houston but you and your spouse are originally from Nebraska, you may decide that it would be pleasant to move back, particularly if many of your oldest and best friends are still there.

Most people would agree that the closest friendships are those made in earlier years. Your basic habit patterns were formed while you were in school and living at home with your parents. It is just possible that you would achieve a greater feeling of being "at home" among those people. Of course, there are still a great many retirees who will say, "I wouldn't go back there for anything in the world!" People differ with respect to how close they want to be to children and grandchildren. Some avoid living near their children because they are preoccupied with the fear of seeming to be meddlesome or dependent. But other things being equal, most people prefer to be near their loved ones.

Planning Your Retirement Lifestyle

Your own plans should be tailored to your needs, and you will have to be the tailor. In planning your retirement lifestyle, you should consider your *finances*, your need for *social integration*, and your *preferred activities.* Also consider *climate, health,* and the *overall quality of your life* from day to day during retirement. If you cannot achieve complete satisfaction in all these categories, you must begin to rank them in importance. The decision to move should be made slowly and deliberately. It is a decision that produces considerable stress, even under good conditions. Both husband and wife should agree before a move is made.

Investigate alternative communities and types of dwellings carefully. Visit different areas. Talk with people who know about the area you are considering. Keep in mind that real estate salesmen are generally too prejudiced to be good advisers in this matter. Beware of package deals; investigate them carefully. One couple I know, after careful investigation, found a very congenial retirement community down south. They visited friends there and everything went well. But then they were encouraged to visit another new colony by a developer; they made an impulsive decision to buy a condominium there. Now, a year later, they are trying to sell the place so they can be among the people they like in the other community.

Perhaps you are not the type who should move into a community created for retired couples. In that case, look around for towns that are not strictly retirement communities but that have a number of congenial people your age, perhaps even a number of "transplants" from other parts of the country.

There is such a wide range of retirement locations

that you should be able to find something suited to your specifications. Obviously, climate is a significant factor, as evidenced by the rapid growth of retired populations in the Sun Belt. On first glance Florida is wall-to-wall condominiums, varying from vast colonies of mobile homes to expensive high-rise apartments to single-family homes often built along a golf course. Southern California has a mixture of everything—pleasant climate, universities, research centers, and cultural and industrial activities. If climate is not an overriding factor, you might consider the numerous condominiums outside major urban areas in such states as Connecticut and New Jersey. These few examples illustrate the range and extremes of retirement locations available.

The following checklist may prove helpful if you are considering moving after retirement. Add any other items that seem appropriate. If, after you have looked over the list, you still are having problems coming to a decision, try ranking the items in order of importance.

REASONS FOR MOVING

1. Financial—lower-cost housing
2. Maintenance—less work around the house and yard
3. Size—smaller place, easier to care for
4. Different community
   Near children
   Near grandchildren
   Near old friends
   Near other retired people
   In a retirement colony
   In old home town or college town

5. Climate—warmer, drier, and so on
6. Activities
   Near ocean, mountains, lakes
   Accessible to theaters, concerts
   Accessible to work desired (not
   necessarily remunerative)

As noted earlier in this chapter, some people approach retirement planning primarily from the perspective of a need for social integration; others approach the problem by thinking about the specific activities they would enjoy doing. Everyone must eventually consider both kinds of planning in order to reconcile one with the other. And, as we already know, both social integration and activities must be compatible with available finances. Having discussed matters of social integration in this chapter, we now turn to ways of thinking about retirement activities.

4

Activities– A Way to Scan the Options

YOUR job regularly claims 50 to 60 hours a week, counting the time required to get to work and back and the time spent on special preparation outside your workplace. When you retire, all at once these hours become available for other activities. That is a lot of time, and you can view it as either a threat or a promise. How you respond depends on your skill in analyzing and planning the use of your time and in adjusting your attitudes toward the expenditure of time once you retire.

By now, you should be familiar with the "segmentation" approach to planning, which you have used in analyzing your financial resources and preferred lifestyle. This approach is no less useful in planning the use of your time. By analyzing the possibilities step by step and by approaching the major questions from several points of view, you can begin to make choices which will lead you to a diversity of activities that will satisfy you in retirement. Your objective should be to give direction to your planning rather than to scatter your shots.

Retirement and New Attitudes About Time

Like most people, you are probably a bit apprehensive about how you will use your time in retirement. For 40 years or more, your self-respect has been tied to breadwinning. Our society expects everyone to *produce* in exchange for material benefits. We punish laziness and reward industry. It should not be surprising, then, that many people experience feelings of guilt and unworthiness when they stop going to work every day. At first, you may feel that you are cheating or "playing hooky" on society. Part of the problem is that society has not yet worked out a plan or discipline to guide the wholly new group of retired people.

I like to remind retirees before these feelings are established that by working all those years, and while usually fulfilling the parallel obligation of raising a family, they have amply paid their debt to society. Having paid their dues fully, they should have a clear conscience.

I remember the refreshing attitude of a farmer friend of mine who retired somewhat before the age of

65. He abandoned his commercial dairy farm and supported himself by selling off pieces of his property, which had greatly appreciated in value through the years. He kept himself busy doing just as he pleased around the farm, taking on repairs and some minor construction tasks. Over his birthday drink at 65, he said, "Well, I've raised my family and now that I'm 65 I can do just as I please." This point of view is entirely justified, and it is one that I commend to everyone.

Once you are free of feelings of unworthiness, you can consider the many positive aspects of retirement. A real sense of enjoyment in retirement can come from the *freedom of choice.* You are clear of the regimentation of the working world. You can take in a ball game if you like. You can linger over a second cup of coffee at breakfast. You can go to the library. You can work in the garden or refinish that old chair you've wanted to work on for years. You can take courses in subjects that have always interested you. The list is endless.

Retirement also brings a refreshing *change of pace.* Usually, it takes quite some time after the moment of retirement to realize that you *have* undergone a change of pace. The realization can be among the most enjoyable ones of your life. You are free of the pressure to get things done within a fixed period of time. Whatever you choose to do, you can do it at your own pace, without any need to hurry. You are through with the insistent ringing of the alarm clock. Breakfast now becomes a pleasant time of day, a time to contemplate what you most want to do with the day.

Still, you need some kind of overall goal and plan for the use of your time. Very few people can be satisfied with short-term activities chosen day by day. The wives of retirees know this well. As one said: "I wish John had something to do. He's cleaned the garage and rearranged his tools ten times this month." They had not bargained for half as much money and twice as much husband.

Later in this chapter I will introduce you to a general plan for analyzing your overall objectives and calculating approximately how many hours in a week you will have available for new, discretionary activities. You can then begin to define these kinds of activities that you will want to pursue in retirement. In that connection, you will be introduced to an approach that I call *field selection and analysis*. This stepwise progression toward defining retirement activities has worked for a great many people, and I trust that it will work for you if you follow each step carefully. I know of no substitute for this kind of segmented planning. *The basis for a satisfactory life in retirement lies in determining what all the options are, deciding which ones to pursue and how to pursue them, and finally acting on these decisions.* With this kind of planning, your new way of life can be very attractive.

Before we begin the field selection process, let us examine a few concepts about personal and career development that should help you feel more confident about enjoying your new freedom. The point is to bring out the various sociological and psychological aspects of retirement within which you will be selecting your fields, and in which you will be living.

Personal Development and Career Development

The career development concept considers a lifetime as a continuous flow of development stages. One of the best-known books on career development,

Eric Erikson's *Childhood and Society*,* divides the life pattern into eight stages, each building on the previous one. Donald Super, in his book on career development,† focuses on the selection and development of a career. I like to think of life and career in terms of five major stages.

The first stage is *preadolescence*. During that time people start school and undertake their first formal learning. Their agenda calls for increasing emancipation from the family, learning the basic skills and disciplines required by society, and learning to relate to peers.

The second major stage, and one about which many books have been written, is *adolescence*. ‡ During adolescence, people begin to make serious career choices and to move concertedly away from dependence on the family.

The next stage is *early career*. Here people begin their working life. They must overcome the problems of adjusting to the regularities of the job and of working in an environment with other people. It is a period of intense learning and development. People begin to move up the career ladder and to develop their full capabilities as workers. Also during this time they are likely to marry and start a family.

Next comes the stage of *career maintenance*. Here people concentrate on furthering their careers and establishing their place in the community. For the first time, they are likely to start saving significant amounts of money and developing hobbies. At the same time,

* Erik H. Erikson, *Childhood and Society* (New York: W. W. Norton, 1963), Parts 1, 5, 6, and 7.
† Donald E. Super, *The Psychology of Careers* (New York: Harper & Row, 1957).
‡ See, for example, Eli Ginzberg, *The Development of Human Resources* (New York: McGraw-Hill, 1966).

they undergo the joys and rigors of raising a family. Their children move into adolescence and then into careers and families of their own.

The fifth stage, one that encompasses many years, is *retirement*. With childrearing and working obligations behind them, retired people encounter freedom of choice, enjoyment of leisure, and new opportunities for self-satisfaction. Usually, there is the need for social reintegration and careful planning for the measured spending of irreplaceable capital.

Personal development and career development should be seen as parallel, lifelong processes. Most of the stages flow into one another. People do not pass abruptly from one phase to the next. Each stage builds on, and is determined largely by, what has preceded it.

Life and career can be seen as a series of roads that fork. At each fork decisions must be made. As you make each decision, your life takes on a different character and direction. Patterns emerge. Remember the old adage: "As the twig is bent, so grows the tree." You choose a certain form of education, decide whom to marry, seek a certain kind of career, and hold a sequence of jobs. Of all the stages faced in life, retirement is perhaps the most precipitous at the onset. The reason is that you are faced with a whole new series of problems and choices—financial, social, geographical, and recreational.

While earlier development stages may slide into one another, retirement really qualifies as an *incident*, with a clear beginning. However, once the initial decisions have been made, retirement becomes an evolutionary process, stretching over many years of changing conditions. People do not simply make decisions once and then carry them out. In the course of retirement there are, inevitably, more forks in the road, with more decisions. We concentrate here on the possibilities for beginning retirement under the best circumstances.

With this perspective as a backdrop, you can begin to make some definite plans for structuring your time. The first step is to determine approximately how much free time you will have. The next step is to analyze your general objectives in using that time. Then you can begin to make some initial choices about activities for retirement. In order to do all this, you will need to study your general objectives carefully, cast them against broad fields of activity, and examine the various organizations related to those fields. Finally, you will make a list of specific activities.

How Much Free Time in Retirement?

At the outset, you should map as clearly as possible the differences between your daily routine in working life and your anticipated routine in retirement. You can then determine how much free time you will have when you retire. The worksheets at the end of this chapter will help you in planning your retirement time. You can make your own set of worksheets from the examples shown.

Use Worksheet No. 8 to list your activities, hour by hour, for a whole working week. If your weeks vary greatly, record two or three, covering as many possible activities that account for your time. Then, using Worksheet No. 9, fill out a weekly schedule eliminating all work activities and all activities involved in preparing for or traveling to and from work. In the spaces previously occupied by work-related activities, simply write "free."

It is important for you to spend as much time as necessary on these schedules. Keep in mind that elimination of regular work is not the only change that will take place when you retire. Depending on the changes in your lifestyle, you may find that much of your routine is altered. For example, if you move from a house to an apartment, you will no longer be spending part of each week working in the yard. Think, too, of new activities that you anticipate. I am not asking you to engage in crystal-ball speculation, but only to document those contrasts that you *know* will pertain. Please fill out the forms now.

I assume that as you read this paragraph you have finished filling out "before and after" weekly schedule sheets. Like most people, you were probably amazed—even a little frightened—at just how much free time you will have in retirement. You looked at all those free spaces in your week and probably said to yourself, "I always knew that there was plenty of free time in retirement, but according to this schedule I'll have even more time than I thought. It comes so suddenly—what, exactly, am I going to do with all that time?" There is a natural tendency to try filling in some of that space, even if only to make guesses about how you will use your newly found hours. Before you get too uncomfortable, let me reassure you. Almost everyone who plans retirement carefully and approaches the question of activities with an open mind finds that the days and weeks are too short instead of too long.

All of us have good and challenging ways to use retirement time. Most of us have more opportunities than we can handle. If you need more reassurance about this, take a few moments to list some of the activities that you enjoy most. Don't bother to categorize the activities or analyze your preferences. Just write down some things that you enjoy. Would you like to have time to take a trip, play cards, or work as a fundraiser for a local charity? Do you want to spend time in the library, take a course, or try the piano again? Before your list has grown very long, you will realize that you cannot do all the things on it. Like most retirees, you will have to make *choices* among activities.

How do you make these choices? You can begin by analyzing your own hierarchy of objectives for using your free time.

Objectives in Using Your Time

In Chapter 1 I introduced the concept of a hierarchy of needs. For planning your retirement time, you should consider three kinds of needs. First and most obviously, you will have to provide for your *subsistence*. Beyond that you have a powerful need for *self-respect*, which comes from social acceptance and admiration by others. Finally, at the highest level of the hierarchy, you need to achieve *self-satisfaction*.

Self-satisfaction comes from the conviction that you are, and are known to be, a worthwhile human being. People most frequently achieve this feeling by doing something concrete, something that has "a bite to it." One person achieves satisfaction by creating a fine piece of furniture. Another achieves satisfaction by doing a worthwhile piece of research. The point is that you need tangible, observable results from your efforts. These results should be a source of pride.

Let us now cast the hierarchy strictly in terms of

your objectives regarding retirement activities. In the discussion of lifestyle in Chapter 3, I outlined the kinds of personal objectives that might pertain here. In the discussion of lifestyle, I suggested that many people approach retirement planning primarily as a means of insuring that they will achieve or maintain *social integration,* a profound need in our culture. Others approach planning primarily as a means of choosing *activities* that will offer monetary or other rewards. Again, those people who look primarily to activities may be motivated by a concern for generating income in retirement or by the need to feel socially productive and worthwhile. Basically, retirement activities can be classified as fulfilling needs that are *social, productive,* or *financial.* Your decisions with respect to these objectives will help give direction to your planning of leisure time.

The decisions you make in preparation for the initial stages of retirement need not be final. Just as conditions have changed throughout your working life, so conditions will change when you are retired. New circumstances will call for revised planning. For now, you should focus on gaining the skills you need for the planning process. My purpose here is to assist you in establishing a solid base for your activities in retirement and to teach you techniques that will allow you to build on current solutions or modify them as your circumstances change.

Social objectives are the overriding concern for at least half of the retiring population. The loss of social integration is among the classic threats of retirement. In one way or another, we hear many retirees say, "I don't feel wanted. I am lonesome. I don't feel that I belong anymore." All such statements generally mean that the retiree desperately needs a replacement for the social acceptance, involvement, and sense of belonging that he previously derived from his job and position in the community. People differ in their particular mixture of needs as they approach retirement, but no one looks easily upon the prospect of increasing social isolation.

Very often, when I ask people what they want to do with their time in retirement, they say, "I don't want to do anything." This statement seems puzzling at first, but I have found that almost always it is a thin disguise for the fact that people are preoccupied with the need to belong to a group or community. Social integration and retirement are not, of course, mutually exclusive, but they often appear to be to retirees. Many people are so worried about remaining close to others that they cannot even consider planning activities for retirement. Yet activities can be a primary means of remaining close to and involved with other people.

Productive objectives include finding activities that are satisfying in themselves, with no financial benefit. You may decide to do things that you really like or things that you feel make a useful contribution to society. Such activities may include working as a volunteer in the community, undertaking a course of study, and improving your skill in a craft for creative satisfaction. Often, this kind of productive activity can be followed into advanced years. Indeed, it may become more important then. I have seen people in their eighties working in thrift shops and hospitals. Many sectors of society need volunteers and provide an attractive opportunity for those who have the luxury of offering their skill and time without pay.

There are, unfortunately, a few skeptics who refuse to consider a new way of life in retirement. They want to continue experiencing the power and the sense of monetary achievement to which they were accustomed. I say unfortunately because such people lead a life of frustration and progressive disengagement from the social mainstream. Once in a great while they get a new job after 65 that is as good or better than the one they previously held. But even for these few the job lasts only five to seven years, still leaving them to face retirement.

Discussing productive objectives, one retired executive who refused to face his new situation told me: "Don't give me that stuff. Volunteer work is for the birds. You don't get paid anything so you don't get any responsibility or results." By contrast, a friend of his became a trustee on the local hospital board and subsequently its chairman. During his tenure, the hospital undertook a substantial building program for new and improved services. Another friend who had been president of a corporation that was "the darling" of Wall Street got on the board of a foundation with considerable capital. He became the driving force in establishing one of the outstanding nonprofit convalescent homes in the country. Once this was accomplished he turned his attention to low-cost housing for the elderly in his town. This involved funding, zoning, taxes, construction, management politics, and all the other functions and problems involved in achieving such a goal. He still found time to sketch and occasionally got a ribbon in one of the local art shows.

By big-business standards, these are peanut operations. However, from the point of view of providing self-satisfaction, they are very successful. Probably just as important, they provide social integration, getting people actively involved in community life, working with many others toward common satisfactory goals.

It is true that not all volunteer jobs can show such tangible results. Most often in volunteer work one starts at the bottom—like the new kid in school—and gradually finds a niche that supplies satisfaction in terms of productivity any social integration within the community. This is the essence of the "quality of life" orientation versus the previous goal-based one.

Financial objectives require working at a job that produces income. If you find it necessary to earn a certain amount of money in order to maintain your desired lifestyle, you will have to structure your time accordingly. But you may also decide to earn money simply becasue you emjoy doing so, because earning has a continuing value for your self-image and self-respect.

Usually, I do not encourage people to work for money in retirement, at least in the beginning, unless it is absolutely necessary. A major reason is that the jobs available to retired people usually offer less authority, less responsibility, and less remuneration than the jobs from which they have retired. Furthermore, as people grow older, their prospects for getting or keeping a paying job diminish. Indeed, by the age of 72, so few people are earning a significant amount of money that the Social Security Administration permits them unlimited earnings without reducing their benefits.

Another reason I do not recommend that retirees seek new jobs immediately is that they often use work as a way of dodging other, potentially more satisfying activities. It is better to come to grips with the decision-making process. If it is possible for you to use your free time to develop new interests and abilities, you should give it a try. Besides being broadening and enlivening, new activities can be fun.

From Objectives to Activities

The problem of deciding how to use retirement time is a new one for mankind, largely because retirement itself is a new phenomenon, less than a century old. Only recently has society begun to dignify the options open to retirees. The social structure has required a time of adjustment. We have always had rules and norms for other stages of life, but not for the retirement stage.

Even now, some sociologists are against the concept of retirement. They note that many professions do not impose retirement on people over 65 who are physically and intellectually able to continue working. They point out, further, that these people often continue happily in their jobs, and render productive service to society for many years. This is certainly true of many doctors and lawyers and of certain other kinds of highly placed professionals and businesspeople. It is also true of many artists, senators, and musicians. But I believe that these exceptions do not disprove the rule: the vast majority of people choose or are forced to retire from their careers.

The point is that society should take steps to improve the quality of life for retired people. The time has passed when we can pack older citizens off to nursing homes just because they have retired from their jobs. Up to now, society's main goal in dealing with retirees has been to give them the financial resources they need (such as social security and pensions) to remain self-supporting. Now it is time for society to focus on psychological and social benefits as well.

Whenever I lecture on retirement, I emphasize the need to facilitate retired people's integration into a satisfactory social scheme. I wish that I could report satisfactory progress on that front, but the fact remains that society is still unprepared to deal with the phenomenon of a lot of retired people over 65 years old. *You* must make these arrangements for yourself, with little help from social institutions. That is why I am writing this book, and why it should be helpful to you.

At this stage of your retirement planning, it is worth your time to reflect at length on the three kinds of personal objectives summarized above. They are not mutually exclusive, to be sure, but as you begin to analyze them, you will move in one direction or another. For now, maybe the most you can do is to weigh the several objectives, asking yourself what your needs are in each of the categories. Then, upon reflection, you should begin to have some notion about which ones are more important. Hold these priorities in mind as you continue your analysis.

The Field Selection Approach to Choosing Activities

Some years ago I worked as a business-management consultant. My company became involved in helping other companies choose avenues of enlargement and diversification. If a client wanted to acquire another company with which it could establish a mutuality of interest and understanding, our job was to guide the client toward a likely choice, compatible with its existing goals, skills, and employees. The same principles that we used there are applicable to your choice of retirement activities. In fact, when you retire, society challenges *you* to diversify. Diversification is the key to successful retirement.

This involves a decision-making system that should by now be familiar and logical to you. The first task is to enumerate a number of fields of activity that appeal to you. You should list as many fields as seem sensible for a thorough exploration of your interests. Then, undertake a preliminary analysis of those fields you have listed. You should be able to list up to seven fields. The next step is to rank the fields according to your degree of interest. You will then analyze thoroughly the field that you have ranked the highest and, finally, select component activities in the field that seem likely to give you the most satisfaction.

One word of caution: this exercise may produce a wide range of options that you have not considered before. Be careful not to lose your sense of reality. It is fine to be interested in many things, but you should not seize upon choices that are impractical. In particular, don't get sidetracked thinking about activities that will require a great deal of training or stamina. For example, it would be unrealistic to work toward a Ph.D. It would probably take you six years, and then you would only be at the start of a new profession. Professors over 70 are a rarity, and teaching is a very hard profession to enter. Be honest with yourself and rule out obvious impracticalities from the beginning. Have no fear—there will be more than enough options available for your consideration.

Listing and Ranking Fields of Interest

As you think about fields, consider the broadest possible categories of activities. There is no rigid definition of "field," but the word is broad enough to include the activities of many functions, individuals, and organizations. The *health* field, for example, includes hospital workers, pharmaceutical employees, surgeons, nurses, technicians, volunteer aides, and so on. Likewise, the field of *education* includes various people, organizations, and activities—teachers, textbook authors, financial administrators, and others.

In order to help you compile a group of fields, I have supplied an arbitrary list below. The list is not exhaustive, for no list could be. Rather, it includes some of the fields I have encountered most frequently.

Possible Fields of Activity

Welfare	Research
Horticulture	Electronics
Sports	Public relations
Music	Retailing
Education	Accounting
Community affairs	Travel
Arts and crafts	Literature

As you prepare your own list, include all those fields that might reasonably provide interesting activities for you, don't worry if the fields seem to be dissimilar. People often "scatter their shots" at this stage of the planning process. You will have an opportunity to scale the list down later.

Again, you should maintain the broadest possible view of each field. People often pick a specific activity or organization in a given field, then work backward to discover what the name of the field might be. That approach places unnecessary limits on the options open to you. There is nothing wrong with entering the decision-making process with some specific activities in mind, as long as you are willing to suspend final choice until you have gone through all the steps. For example, if you think automatically of volunteering for hospital work, you should broaden the category to include welfare work, medical endeavors, and community affairs. The point is to find out what *else* in those fields may appeal to you.

Try to list at least seven possible fields of interest. You may find it helpful here to review your past experience. Think about the jobs you have had or the jobs you know something about. Make a note of those you like and summarize what appeals to you about them. You should also consider non-job-related activities. List hobbies and subjects that you enjoy reading about. Career counselors often suggest that their clients take psychological interest tests. However, I have found that these tests are of limited usefulness to people like you, because you have lived long enough and have enough experience to know what you like and what you don't like, what you can do and what you cannot do.

Once you have prepared your list of fields, you will need to analyze and rank them in order of the attractiveness each holds for you. To assist you in this, I suggest that you specify several kinds of information about each field. First, specify the *organizations* that operate in that field. Second, enumerate as many possible *products and services* associated with the field. Finally, list as many *specific functions (jobs)* that you know exist within the field. Here are two examples to help you begin.

Field: Education

Organizations

College
University
Trade school
High school
YMCA
Art or music school

Products and Services

Diplomas
Degrees
Specific skills
Certification
Research

Specific Functions (Jobs)

Administration
President
Treasurer
Building and grounds
Public relations
Fund raising
Teaching
Lab and field research
Student

Field: Horticulture

Organizations

Commercial nursery
Lawn or tree care company
Garden club
Florist

Products and Services

Flowers
Vegetables
Greenhouse plants
Specialty plants
New species

Specific Functions (Jobs)

Sales
Accounting
Purchasing
Noncommercial activities
Experimentation
Running a greenhouse
Raising specimen plants
Hybridizing
Running a local garden club
Participating in a national garden club
Participating in specialty garden clubs

Naturally, in making such lists, you will not know all you need to know about every field. Don't worry about this now. Later you will have an opportunity to delve deeply into one or two fields. For now, do the best you can.

In order to rank these fields, refer to Worksheet No. 10. Two such sheets will help you analyze as many as eight fields. Once you have listed them, underline at least one item of major interest in each of the three categories. In other words, for each field underline one kind of organization, one kind of product or service, and at least one specific function or job. This process will help you pinpoint interests and activities within each field.

In one of the specific case studies recounted in the next chapter, you will see that Robert ultimately chose the field of education. The example above comes from his own experience. At this stage of his planning, he underlined the *university* as a preferred organization. Under products and services, he underlined *degrees*, *specific skills*, and *research*. Under specific functions, he underlined *lab and field research* and *student*.

In order to be sure that you include all the products, services, and activities related to a given field, think in terms of the four major functions in most organizations: *engineering, production, marketing,* and *finance.* These categories may apply more directly to business organizations than to others, but they are useful guideposts for identifying the major components of any field. There are, of course, many subfunctions within an organization or field, and within these there are many sub-subfunctions.

Ranking the Fields

When you have filled out all the categories and underlined your major interests, you will probably find that some fields seem more appealing than others and that you still have much to learn about them. You are now ready to analyze the fields and to weigh them against one another.

How do you investigate the opportunities available within a field? There are many sources of additional information. You can do library work on the subject, go on field trips, or meet with practitioners in the field. Almost every field fits in with some industrial or professional association which can be a rich source of information about the products, services, and activities concerned. Your local library probably has a directory of associations.

Once you have gathered enough preliminary information to isolate one or two fields of special interest, you can begin to do some deeper research. Again, you should use library, professional, and personal resources, even if you are considering only the informal or hobbyist activities in that field. At this point it may be necessary to spend a significant amount of time on library research or to pay a personal visit to an appropriate professional or trade association. People in those offices dispense information freely. In my experience, people are the most informative resource. Do not hesitate to establish a wide range of contacts among people working in the field that interests you. Ask them to review all the products, services, organizations, and activities involved in their field.

In the course of your research, you will begin to form a preliminary opinion about whether the field is (1) as interesting as you thought and (2) appropriate to your background and skills. This is important. If the field becomes *less* attractive to you on either basis, lower its ranking in your tables and begin to investigate the field that carries the next highest ranking. Do not be discouraged if a field appears to lose appeal. You may have to change your focus several times before you find a field that stands up well under careful and deep analysis.

Choosing the Right Activities

If you analyze the fields carefully, you will probably find a number of job-related activities that are "still in the running" after the obviously inappropriate activities have been eliminated. No one can give you a scientific mechanism for choosing among the remaining activities. I suggest that you hold on to all your worksheets as you go through the process of changing your mind and refocusing your attention. New evidence inevitably comes to light as time goes by. You may even have to rerank your fields. Remember, too, to keep your focus practical. It is very important to choose something that is interesting to you, regardless of whether it relates directly to the career from which you are retiring.

Worksheet No. 11 will help you match a specific activity in a field against the way you like to work and some of the things you like to do.

Every specialty within a field requires knowledge and ability as well as interest. It is entirely possible that you will be interested in a field for which you have no background or credentials. Be honest with yourself about this. Analyze your abilities as carefully as you have analyzed your fields of interest. Ask yourself these questions: Do you have the prerequisites for entering the field in any capacity? Do you have the qualifications for your chosen specialty within the field? If you do not have the qualifications now, how long would it take you to acquire them?

All the above questions pertain to *entering* a field initially. You must also consider the personal attributes and qualifications required for *remaining* in the field once you have achieved entry. Do you have the physical stamina, manual dexterity, reflexes and coordination, intellectual and analytical ability, or creative ingenuity to work successfully in the specialty you have chosen? At this point you cannot know about your performance for sure. But if you strongly suspect that you will not be able to qualify over a period of time, it really does not matter whether you have the interest or the entry requirements. You should not enter a field in which you are likely to fail after a time. To do so is frustrating and ultimately disappointing.

New interests and ambitions are the substance of affirmative retirement. Unrealistic ambitions are a sure basis for disappointment. You must try to locate yourself suitably between the unfettered imagination of new opportunities and the realistic appraisal of your possibilities for performance. Between these extremes lies the promise of social integration, productive activity, and perhaps, continued employment. The main purpose of the field selection and analysis process is to help you discover regular, major activities that will serve you in retirement. The process is not limited to jobs and employment; it is equally useful in helping you choose hobbies and avocations. Use its power to find activities that will play a minor part in your week but that will enrich your life and give you the opportunity to have some fun.

No two people move through the field selection and analysis process exactly the same way. And, surely, no two people ever design identical retirement plans for themselves. Affirmative retirement is a highly personal prescription. Only you can decide on satisfying ways to use some of the best years of your life.

WORKSHEET NO. 8
WEEKLY SCHEDULE BEFORE RETIREMENT

	Hour	Mon.	Tues.	Wed.	Thurs.	Fri.	Sat.	Sun.
A.M.	6–7:00							
	7–8:00							
	8–9:00							
	9–10:00							
	10–11:00							
	11–12:00							
P.M.	12–1:00							
	1–2:00							
	2–3:00							
	3–4:00							
	4–5:00							
	5–6:00							
	6–7:00							
	7–8:00							
	8–9:00							
	9–10:00							
	10–11:00							

WORKSHEET NO. 9
WEEKLY SCHEDULE AFTER RETIREMENT

	Hour	Mon.	Tues.	Wed.	Thurs.	Fri.	Sat.	Sun.
A.M.	6–7:00							
	7–8:00							
	8–9:00							
	9–10:00							
	10–11:00							
	11–12:00							
P.M.	12–1:00							
	1–2:00							
	2–3:00							
	3–4:00							
	4–5:00							
	5–6:00							
	6–7:00							
	7–8:00							
	8–9:00							
	9–10:00							
	10–11:00							

WORKSHEET NO. 10
FIELD SELECTION AND ANALYSIS

Field: _____
Products and Services   *Specific Functions (Jobs)*

Organizations

Field: _____
Products and Services   *Specific Functions (Jobs)*

Organizations

Field: _____
Products and Services   *Specific Functions (Jobs)*

Organizations

Field: _____
Products and Services   *Specific Functions (Jobs)*

Organizations

WORKSHEET NO. 11
CRITERIA FOR
SELECTING AN ACTIVITY

Working	Like	Indifferent	Dislike
Outdoors			
Indoors			
At a desk			
Moving Around			
With people			
Influencing people			
With figures			
With words			
With hands			
With mechanical things			
With details			
With tangible things			
With ideas or concepts			
In engineering			
In production			
In marketing			
In finance			
In administration			

5

Some Specific Cases

Now that you know something about financial planning, social planning, and the selection of activities, you may find it helpful to read about how other people have applied these techniques to achieve satisfactory arrangements in retirement. Naturally, I must disguise these case studies slightly by changing names and certain minor details.

The Demarests and the Strongs

I'm going to begin with parallel histories of two different couples because I want you to see that, even though geographical and financial circumstances may be the same for two couples at the point of retirement, they may differ quite significantly in the selection of social objectives. Their objectives led these two couples to divergent choices in retirement.

Al and Mary Demarest lived in the same fine home in the Boston suburbs for 22 years. I met them about three months after Al's retirement. Although he hadn't talked about it much, Al had discovered that he wasn't really happy in retirement. He had done a reasonably good job of analyzing his financial circumstances but was only beginning to wrestle with the problems of activities and social integration. Financially, things were a little tighter than he and Mary had expected. They realized that they could get by in their community if they were especially careful about expenditures, but inflation was beginning to leave them feeling strapped most of the time. They didn't like the feeling of having to watch their money so closely in order to get by from one month to the next.

At about the same time, in another suburb of Boston, my old friend Jack Strong retired from his company at age 65. He and his wife were frank to admit that they had given little thought to exactly how they would use their retirement years, but they had always been confident that they would enjoy the time immensely. I had dinner with Jack and Vivian about two weeks after Jack's farewell party at the office, and I was struck by how similar their circumstances were to the Demarests'.

A superficial examination of these two couples showed many points of correspondence. Both lived in three- or four-bedroom houses, with rather extensive grounds, in relatively affluent neighborhoods. All four people were bright, optimistic, and in good health. Both families had a reasonable amount of money at their disposal in the form of savings, accumulated capital gains, annuities, and pensions. Even so, both were beginning to wonder whether they could maintain their standard of living comfortably in their present locations. Both couples had children and grandchildren, all of whom had settled outside New England.

In my role as informal adviser to the Demarests and the Strongs, I decided to focus on their financial pressures first. In both cases, we determined that on the open market, their houses, both fully paid for, were worth $70,000 to $75,000 each. Believe it or not, neither Al nor Jack had stopped to realize what that meant. A house represents tied-up capital, producing no income. In fact, their houses not only were holding money out of circulation but were costing money in the form of taxes and maintenance.

In each case, I suggested that they consider selling the house to free up capital and then transferring that capital to the production of income. Both couples readily agreed and sold their houses within three months. After commissions and associated expenses, each realized about $65,000, for a profit of about $30,000. At this point you may be thinking that they had to bear some heavy capital gains taxes. That is not so. Each couple reinvested in another house and took advantage of all the tax breaks available to people over 65. The tax on their profit was minimal.

Before we go any further, let's look at how the financial outlook of both couples was affected by the sale of their homes. Expressed in round numbers, here are the benefits to each family:

$65,000 capital, earning interest at 7 percent	$4,500
Real estate tax savings	2,200
Utilities	1,200
Maintenance and repairs	900
Effective increase in annual income, before securing new living space	$8,800

At the time of these transactions, a 7 percent rate of interest after taxes appeared reasonable. Different rates may prevail today. Also, note that the total effect on income must be reduced by the fact that each couple needed a new place to live. As things turned out, the Demarests and the Strongs each invested approximately $35,000 in a new residence. In other words, the capital freed by the sale of their houses was reduced by half.

While their houses were on the market, I talked with both couples about various plans for relocation. The remarkable parallels between the two families continued. Neither couple really wanted to leave New England. They discussed freely the pros and cons of different geographic locations and decided that, even though it was not absolutely necessary to remain in the Boston area, they would explore that alternative among others in New England.

Neither couple felt that they needed a large house or grounds, but both were unwilling to consider a significant reduction in their standard of living. They wanted to be able to travel and to enjoy various forms of local recreation, including club memberships; and they wanted to be able to move about in society comfortably without undue concern for budgetary limitations. Both couples had enjoyed the seasonal changes of the Northeast, but they had found it desirable to go to Florida or the Caribbean every winter for a few weeks.

A preliminary investigation indicated that because the two couples no longer needed to be close to good schools or to commutation services, they could acquire either smaller houses or condominiums for $30,000 to $50,000, depending on the area and the size of the dwelling. Knowing this, the Demarests and the Strongs had some other decisions to make.

Should they remain as close to their original homes as possible, or should they consider moving to other towns? Faced with this question, both couples began to ask themselves about their social objectives—their need for social integration. At this point, the Demarests and the Strongs begin to show some significant differences.

The Demarests had lived in their suburban community for many years and had become very active in the local golf club and in community affairs; they were tied socially and organizationally to a great many people in the area. They concluded that they wanted to relocate in the same vicinity. It was important to them to continue to feel part of the establishment there.

The Strongs had moved to their community only six years before, although they had lived in the greater Boston area for 25 years. Their social life never really took hold in the community. Jack did not play golf or engage in other activities that provided social contact. Vivian had had some difficulty making new friends, partly because she felt that many of the local activities were dominated by younger women. Another problem was that they lived in a highly mobile neighborhood. Young families moved in and out quickly as their companies transferred them from one place to another. It should come as no surprise, then, that Jack and Vivian Strong decided to look further afield for a place to settle down in retirement.

The two couples gave serious thought to the question of living in a home with grounds versus buying a condominium or renting an apartment. I was interested in their analysis, because both couples enjoyed plants and gardening very much. Both had always employed gardening services to handle the heavy work in their yards, but the men enjoyed puttering in the flowers and shrubs, and the women took special delight in cultivating house plants. Neither couple wanted to continue the expense of a gardener.

In thinking about this question, the Demarests decided that they would prefer to have a smaller house with a small yard. Their outdoor gardening was so important to them that they felt they would miss it badly if they didn't have grounds of their own. If the yard were small enough, and reasonably well landscaped to begin with, they would enjoy doing the outdoor work themselves.

The Demarests found a small, charming house within a few miles of their old home. Once part of a larger estate, it had very little property directly attached to it, but the plantings were imaginatively arrayed and thoroughly established. They came to call their place a doll house, because it had only one bedroom and a small den. Still, they felt it was more than enough for the two of them.

The Strongs came to a very different conclusion. They decided that it wasn't the work of gardening they enjoyed so much as the pleasure of seeing the end result. Both were enthusiastic about trees, flowering shrubs, and spring bulbs, but neither really wanted to do the elbow work necessary to bring all of that about. For them, a well-landscaped condominium with the outdoor services managed entirely by others seemed a good solution. The Strongs readily sacrificed any possible pleasures of outdoor gardening and, at the same time, surrendered all the maintenance problems that go with owning a home. They were relieved to realize that in their new location they would not have to build up a "stable" of reliable service people. They would not have to swing into action themselves every time something needed fixing. They would settle for their house plants and let the condominium management take care of just about everything else.

For the Strongs, the condominium had one other valuable advantage. It would help solve their social problems. Most of the people in the condominium development were retired, and the community placed much emphasis on organizing and publicizing social activities. There was a swimming pool, a central entertainment hall for parties and lectures, and a group of nearby stores that practically served as a private shopping center. Frequent cocktail parties and outings allowed established residents to meet the newcomers and to quickly build them into the local social structure. Like the Demarests, the Strongs invested about $35,000 in their new quarters.

A year after my planning sessions with the Strongs and the Demarests, I attended two cocktail parties— one at each home. At the Demarests' party, which was fairly small because of their restricted space, I mingled with some of their best and oldest friends. Still, there were a few new faces—including people who had recently moved into the neighborhood—and I was glad to see them there. Al told me that when everything was said and done, the switch to a smaller house had freed up several thousand dollars of capital. Still, he was not thinking particularly of the increased income or lowered expenses, but rather of the net result—the feeling of being much better off financially.

The Demarests' new, smaller house, it seemed, was virtually maintenance free. Mary was delighted with the reduced burden of housework. Proudly, they showed me that they had spent part of their new-found freedom working outdoors, most notably in executing two magnificent flower beds in the front yard. Mary pointed out that even the plantings were not expensive: many had been clipped and transplanted from the gardens of old friends, eager to do their part in warming the new home. Both still saw their old friends frequently, perhaps more frequently than ever before, and it was clear to me that Al and Mary Demarest were having fun in retirement.

The cocktail party at the Strongs' condominium was a distinct contrast to the one at the Demarests' house. Here were almost all new faces. In fact, I believe that I was the only person there who had known the Strongs longer than a year. Jack and Vivian were perfect as host and hostess, more outgoing than I had ever seen them. The party moved freely from the house to a magnificently maintained flagstone patio, midway between the pool and the house. Jack was proud and relieved to tell me that he was doing better financially than he had thought he would. The combination of the lower investment in the condominium and the lower taxes and maintenance had improved his financial position by more than $3,000 a year. In terms of lifestyle, he was extremely happy. The condominium management took over all maintenance chores formerly left to him, and relieved him of concern for such things as securing the services of a snowplow to clear his parking area and sidewalk.

Jack didn't make any boasts about his social adjustment, but the success was apparent. He chatted freely with people and laughed easily. Vivian admitted that at first she had had entirely too much time on her hands. Even though she was meeting new people, she felt idle, sometimes for days at a stretch. She resolved that by volunteering as an aide in a nearby hospital. There she met a group of women who invited her to join the hostess committee for community events—cocktail parties, amateur theater, and so forth. Even though I knew the answer, I asked Vivian if she was having fun. She looked around a bit and said, "Bob, just look at all these people. There must be 40 here. All I can say is that a year ago Jack and I probably couldn't have made a decent guest list of 14."

The Demarests and the Strongs did not make the same choices, but they went through the same process, and both achieved satisfactory arrangements for their retirement. There is no absolute formula for doing this, but I want to reiterate that in order to derive a personal solution, each couple had to carry out a basic financial analysis first.

This case study has focused on the solution to the problem of home ownership and geographical location. Again, I emphasize that these financial and geographical concerns cannot be analyzed in isolation from the need for social integration. I am more and more convinced that social integration has been grossly underrated in the advice given to retirees. This may be because financial problems are so specific and can be analyzed so precisely. When we start to talk about social integration, we are completely out of the statistical realm. It is a difficult and slippery problem to deal with.

To understand your social needs, you must think long and hard about your own habits and preferences—in short, about your own social lifestyle as you would have it. In the end, your solution must be a global one, encompassing a mix of financial, personal, and social objectives. The Demarests and the Strongs achieved that kind of global solution for themselves. But even knowing that, and even though I was involved in the reorganization of their lives, I still could not tell you how much of their success was dependent on financial arrangement and how much on social integration.

Geoffrey Cartwright

I want to share Geoffrey Cartwright's case with you because in so many respects it is a classic. His situation and perspective have appeared again and again in cases that have come to my attention. The first thing that was typical about Geoffrey was that he came to retirement consultation only reluctantly. His family pressed him to do it because they were tired of having him "moping around the house" and because a friend of his had been helped by a similar consultation. Let me give you some of his background.

After graduating from college, Geoffrey obtained a master's degree in history and began work toward his doctorate. Then his father died. As an only child, Geoffrey felt it was necessary, at least for the time being, to go home and take over the family business. As it turned out, he never returned to school. The business was a medium-sized retail store with a considerable amount of adjoining business real estate. As things worked out, Geoffrey discovered that he had a definite talent for business. He particularly liked retailing and over the years was able to generate adequate profits to meet his needs. He especially liked being his own boss.

Gradually, the area around his business property deteriorated. A year before I saw Geoffrey, and just as he was beginning to wonder about his own retirement, all his land and buildings, together with the surrounding area, were expropriated for a major urban redevelopment project. The settlement on his real estate was roughly equivalent to a satisfactory pension he might have received had he been with a large corporation all those years. Geoffrey was beginning to feel cautious, and although he was only 61 he didn't dare risk investing this capital in a new business elsewhere. In truth, his retail business had not been an outstanding success (it had shown no growth over the last ten years). He knew that, under the best of circumstances, it might take him four or five years in a new location to begin developing satisfactory profits. At his age, and recognizing that his capital was irreplaceable, he took a cautious stance.

When his business finally closed, the event was almost a relief. He told me that the "nagging fear" had started almost five years before. Eventually, he admitted to me that although he normally was a very practical, commonsense person, he was almost immobilized when it came to planning for his own retirement. With only thinly veiled desperation, he told me, "Oh, I've looked at and considered all sorts of things, but nothing seems right."

Getting Geoffrey to start planning (without mentioning that dirty word) turned out to be easier than I thought. I guided him first into the specifics of financial planning. His income was several thousand dollars short of what he would need in retirement. One problem was that, as a late father, he still had two children who would be in college for the next two and four years respectively. His other three children had already graduated. My formula for the gradual use of irreplaceable capital came as a revelation to Geoffrey. When we applied the formula, he felt more comfortable about using some of his capital during the immediate years ahead, when his needs would be great. He had been using this capital anyway for the last year, but it had greatly contributed to his worries about going broke.

By the time of our second meeting, Geoffrey was much more relaxed. He was no longer afraid that he would have to move or cut back significantly on his standard of living. Geoffrey didn't really want to change his social environment. He had lived in a city in the mid-South all his life and greatly enjoyed meeting with old friends. Furthermore, several of his children still were located in the area. He felt no need for any further or changed social integration.

Having allayed his worst fears about the future of his finances, we turned to questions of the use of his time. Community affairs and nonprofit organizations didn't interest him much. He had always made the charitable contributions that were expected of him as a member of the community, but that's as far as it went. Geoffrey had never been involved in volunteer work and had little interest in starting this kind of activity now. Instead, he insisted that even though his store and properties had been liquidated, what he really liked most was business.

At our third meeting I said to Geoffrey, "Since you've decided that you want to be gainfully employed, why don't you tell me exactly what you want to do?" He replied, "I wish I knew. I've considered many things." His problem was that he didn't know how to begin the exploration. During the rest of that session, we explored the field selection and analysis approach previously defined. We looked over a résumé that he had prepared, showing his educational and professional background. From that, we got clues about the things which he had enjoyed most. Then he made a list of jobs he had heard about that he thought might be interesting. Our goal here was to list every activity that he had ever thought about with any degree of interest. "You see," he said, "I've been all over the lot." He was right about that, and now he recognized it. I gave him a "homework assignment." I wanted him to organize the list into fields of activity.

At the next meeting, he presented a list of seven fields he had developed: education, literature, publicity, real estate, retailing, retail store in the same line of business, and retailing franchise.

I told him that he had done a good job on his homework. Each field on the list met our criteria in that it had multiple institutions associated with it, many broad functions, and many kinds of products or services. I could have quibbled with him about putting retailing in his list three times, but it was unnecessary, because the important objectives had been achieved. He had listed the parameters of his present interest. The list constituted a base from which to start the discrimination process. His next task was to rank the fields and select a high-priority field for further analysis.

When I asked him to try that, he said, "I don't know which ones I really prefer. That's the trouble." There was nothing to do but start a discussion of each field separately: why he had chosen it as a field, what he liked about it, what it would do for him, and what opportunities it presented for him. I had to get him thinking in personal and practical terms about each field on the list. For two hours I engaged him in conversation in which our primary goals were discrimination and ranking. Here are some of the highlights.

Education

Geoffrey had grown up in a college town in the mid-South and had had considerable success in his education. He liked the university atmosphere and once had considered an academic career, which he judged to be a low-pressure occupation that carried considerable status. He had put education on his list because he had considered the possibility of being a college or prep school president. As we talked about it, this sounded appealing but he did not have a Ph.D. or any background experience in running such an institution. Without much struggle, Geoffrey recognized that it was simply wishful thinking to expect an offer to serve as college president somewhere.

What about some other administrative job at a prep school or college? Here, he was on a bit sounder ground. He had some administrative experience and had done some public relations writing along the way. Early in his career, he had done some free-lance work for a firm whose primary business was fund raising. He knew something about construction and building maintenance and had always managed a group of people. It appeared to us both that there might be some realistic prospects in work as an administrative assistant in public relations, fund raising, or the building and grounds department of a school.

Geoffrey decided to table this option for the time being. He admitted that, as he considered such positions, they might not give him a status comparable to that of his college professor friends. He also suspected that, once having acquired such a job, he might not be too keen on the type of work involved. It was important for him to have a job in which he could feel strongly motivated.

Teaching also appealed to him, more for the status than for the intrinsic satisfactions of teaching. At his age, he felt that he had become a bit out of touch with the younger generation; he knew, furthermore, that most schools were working under extreme budget restrictions. He thought the prospects were very slim that any school in his area would hire him at his age.

In sum, for Geoffrey the field of education did not seem to be a very practical consideration. Nevertheless, instead of removing it from the list, he decided to keep it, and gave it the lowest rank, No. 7. There were, after all, some remote prospects, and it was just possible that no other field would prove more promising.

Literature

The field of literature didn't produce much for Geoffrey. To be sure, he had read widely all his life. He liked thinking about the sales and promotion aspects of the publishing industry, but he couldn't figure out any slot where he would fit, except as a salesman in a bookstore. This, he felt, would be too restrictive and wouldn't pay very much. He decided to put the bookstore possibility aside and come back to it later if he had to. Then it occurred to him that he might consider buying into a bookstore, even though it would mean risking some of his capital. In the end, he felt that this field had better prospects for him than education, so he ranked it No. 6.

Publicity

Because he had done some public relations writing and liked the whole challenge of promotion, Geofrey thought he might be a good director of a trade association. He knew some directors and felt that this possibility warranted further investigation. Because he still had several more fields to examine, he wasn't sure exactly where to rank it. As a guess, he ranked it No. 3.

Real Estate

Throughout his business life Geoffrey had managed his own property investments. He had even gone so far as to get a license as a real estate broker. But the work didn't particularly appeal to him, and he thought that in the current depressed market he wouldn't make a satisfactory income selling real estate. We discussed the prospects of managing a condominium or apartment building, but this did not appeal to him at all. He felt that the only thing that would please him would be to work as a commissioned agent for some real estate company. He ranked the field No. 5.

Retailing

On his own, Geoffrey realized that all the remaining fields had something in common. He was tempted to group them together for analysis, but I asked him to consider each one separately, because there were some minor differences. Retailing seemed a bit too broad to be considered one field. Because it was so general, and as such yielded no practical prospect, he ranked it No. 4.

Geoffrey's interest in retailing came down to the fact that he had liked all aspects of running his own retail store. He said that he would go right back into the same business in a new location if he dared risk the capital. Then we wondered together: How close to this field could he get? Geoffrey considered the possibility of getting a job as a manager of a store in the same line. Next, he thought about forming a partnership with other experienced retailers to establish a new business. Another possibility was to buy into an existing partnership.

This led us to talk about taking a franchise in a business similar to the one he had run through the years. I pointed out that this would require a lot less capital than building his own store and that the franchisor would supply him with a lot of services and market studies to reduce his risk. As a result, he ranked a retail franchise as his No. 1, field. At this point, by reviewing the group of fields, Geoffrey found that he could rank this as No. 1 and the rest of the fields got lost in the shuffle. He no longer felt that he needed to bother with ranking. Geoffrey began to show some enthusiasm for the future. The very next day he was off to seek more information from the retail franchise association in his area.

After reviewing the types of franchise operations in which he might be interested, Geoffrey visited some of them. As it turned out, he did not end up with a franchise outlet of his own; rather he took a job as regional manager for the franchisor. This position made use of Geoffrey's experience and abilities beautifully. He is still looking around for just the right franchise, but even if none becomes available he is well situated.

Felix and Marge Houton

I have told you that, at the point of retirement, the change in your life can be considered to be an incident—an important change that can come upon you quite suddenly. Inevitably, one day you are working at your job and the next day you are technically retired. I have told you also that retirement is an evolutionary process that requires continued analysis and adaptation after the incident itself. The case of Felix and Marge Houton illustrates the difference between the incident and the ongoing process.

Felix and Marge both went to Ivy League colleges and subsequently raised their family in New England. When Felix was in his late forties, he moved up the corporate ladder very quickly and eventually assumed a high-level position at his company headquarters in the Midwest. There, he prospered in his career until he retired.

Financially, the Houtons were well-off at the point of retirement. Felix had a good pension and had saved consistently. His company stock options turned out to be extremely profitable. Translating their holdings into income for retirement, the Houtons found that they had more than enough to live comfortably and to leave their children a considerable estate.

Upon retirement, Felix and his wife decided to move back to the town in New England where they had raised their family. They felt that they still had roots there and wanted to be near old friends. They sold their big house in the Midwest and bought a much smaller but adequate one back in New England. Realizing that they did not want to be idle, they began to look at fields of activity. Gardening was their first choice, and travel was found to be an interesting avocation for them both. When they looked for their new home, they specified that it should be possible to add a greenhouse, which they installed with all the latest heating, ventilating, and lighting equipment for the care of plants. As soon as they were settled, they began annual trips during the dark, cold months of January and February.

On the face of it, the Houtons' retirement sounds ideal, and it was—for a time. If retirement were just an incident, and if all factors remained stable thereafter, they couldn't have been better situated. The Houtons were perceptive enough, however, to realize that retirement is also a process, and that conditions change over a period of time. Fortunately, the Houtons were adaptable.

It didn't take long for them to realize that their need for social integration was not being fulfilled. Some of their old friends had retired but had then moved away from New England. They were sad to learn that other friends had died. Still others remained in the workforce, moving busily in the swing of things during the week and then spending very active social weekends. It appeared that the Houtons, by virtue of their own circumstances, were on a different wavelength from the people they knew in the community. And once the novelty wore off, working in the greenhouse seemed to be a lonely occupation.

Then the evolutionary, adaptive process began. Felix joined the local men's garden club, where he made some new friends who shared his interests. He took a special interest in begonias and began to develop expertise and special skills in growing new, unusual varieties. Subsequently, he became president of the garden club and later took active part in regional and national garden club affairs. This not only opened up a whole new social life for him and Marge but also gave him the satisfaction of winning blue ribbons and awards for outstanding plants he had developed. Marge took a positive role in the women's garden club and became active as a volunteer in the community thrift shop. Along the way, she expanded her circle of bridge players.

Today, as they approach their mid-70s, Felix and Marge feel that they have done pretty well. They know that, in future years, health may bring new problems and cause them to make additional changes. But until health or other circumstances require new adaptations, they are satisfied with the quality of their lives in retirement.

John and Johanna Barton

Anyone, including John Barton himself, would tell you that during the years leading up to retirement his life was more than satisfactory in every way. He had a good job in upper-middle management working for a large corporation in Southern California. There, he was responsible for mass movement of goods. He supervised the work of many people and did it well. It was the kind of work that he liked, for it required meticulous attention to many details. It was not a job that called for much conceptual or theoretical thinking, but John didn't like that kind of work anyway.

The Bartons had raised two children, who did well at school, secured good positions, and began to form their own families. As so often happens, the children both set up their homes in distant cities, which meant that they were able to see their parents only infrequently. Nevertheless, the Bartons kept their large house in a prosperous exurban area, with several acres of ground. As he approached retirement, John came to think of the house, and particularly the grounds, as an unnecessary burden. In years past, he and the kids had pretty much taken care of the place by themselves. John began to think vaguely of selling the place.

John was a gregarious person who enjoyed his friends immensely. He played poker and pinochle regularly with members of his Masonic lodge. He had a strong interest in music and enjoyed playing the guitar, especially on those occasions when he could find another musician to play with him. Johanna Barton was not nearly as gregarious as her husband. She seemed to be completely satisfied to stay home most of the time. It wasn't that she resisted social activity, but rather that she didn't seek it. In that regard, she had always simply gone along with the wishes of her husband and children.

As John approached retirement, he began to show some signs of concern and uncertainty. His older son tried to get him to do some planning, but John was reluctant to discuss it with his son or anyone else. The problem, I think, was that John was not prepared to accept the idea of being old. He utterly rejected the idea of "being put on the shelf." He once said, "I'm not going to sit on the porch doing nothing like those old guys." Financially, John was more than capable of satisfying his needs. He had a good pension and had accumulated sufficient savings to be sure of maintaining his standard of living.

In all these respects, then, John Barton was not the sort of person you would expect to have trouble making the transition to retirement. The point here is that a successful life up to the time of retirement does not guarantee a smooth transition. Psychological as well as practical considerations can complicate the picture considerably. Who would have predicted that the first eight years of John's retirement would be characterized by groping frustration?

At the time he turned 65, John was in very good health and was undeniably valuable to his company. The officers of the company asked him to stay on part time as a consultant. John accepted because he had no other plan in mind, but he soon found this intolerable. For years, he had been used to wielding authority; in his new position as consultant, he was no longer able to tell people what to do. The company had tried to put him in a planning role, but he felt lost in that capacity. The arrangement lasted only a year.

At that point, he decided to make a radical change. He couldn't be idle, so he took a job in a local hardware store. Even in the store, his leadership capabilities were soon recognized by everyone else working there. Employees began to look to him to solve their problems in the store. Finding answers seemed easy to John, and he was both liked and respected on the job. The only problem was that this job meant long hours on his feet, which he couldn't take any more. He got tired and irritable after a year and resigned. Next, John looked into the franchise business and seriously considered buying a laundromat.

As he thought about it, though, it didn't seem like much fun; besides, he was reluctant to risk so much of his capital.

Without a regular job, John began to have more and more trouble just filling his time meaningfully. He began to take more interest in his Masonic lodge and became its treasurer. The detail work took up a lot of his time, but not all of it. More often than before, he began to accept invitations to play golf or poker with his cronies. In a desultory way, he still played the guitar and tried to develop an interest in some of the newer styles of music. In a weak moment, he admitted to his wife that all this was just "busy work." Nothing had "a real bite to it."

By this time, John's reluctance to plan was beginning to get in his way. He knew that he had to do something about his living quarters, because he was no longer motivated to keep up with the maintenance of the house and yard. Also, he and Johanna did not need so much space. He approached the problem of relocation in the same piecemeal, try-this-try-that fashion that he had used in other affairs. Over the next few years, the Bartons sold their big house and bought and sold two successively smaller ones in different communities. Each location left something to be desired in terms of social contact, especially for John. Finally, again almost by trial and error, they bought a condominium in a retirement colony.

In the beginning, a retirement colony was the last thing that John Barton would have considered. He came to it by degree and by necessity. In this colony, the buyer had to be over 55 with no children under 18. Almost as soon as the Bartons moved in, some of the advantages of this place for them became apparent.

First of all, there were no longer any maintenance or repair problems. Also, there was an active social program built around an attractive entertainment hall and swimming-pool complex. John soon became friendly with a man who played the piano, and the two of them began to play together several mornings a week in the empty community hall. In due course, they were joined by a drummer and a saxophone player, and the four of them got into the habit of regular sessions.

The social program of the community included at least one "happy hour" cocktail party a week. Eventually, the host and hostess at one of these parties asked John and his fellow musicians to play. Their music turned out to be a popular addition to the party, and they played at still more as time went on. From there, they pursued a series of engagements to play at parties for the Masons, the Kiwanis Club, and other organizations. That led to a date to play for a local school dance, where they were paid for the first time. They made $100 for the evening. No one in the group was doing it for money, of course, but they all derived a peculiar satisfaction from receiving pay for what had started out to be a hobby.

Later, with all the parties taking place during Christmas holidays, John and his fellow musicians sometimes made as much as $1,000 a month. Most important, they found that they could get enough engagements to keep as busy as they wanted to be. This required, of course, that they practice together regularly, and John particularly enjoyed the discipline of the practice schedule. Here, in the condominium community, John was finding the satisfaction he had been seeking for eight years. He felt productive and wanted. He was making good use of his own talents. Today, at 80 years of age, John is enjoying his affirmative retirement.

John might have achieved his satisfactory solution in two years instead of eight if he had planned his retirement before going into it. The field selection approach would have led him to music as a major interest from the outset. John's son, who is a very good planner, later told me that he understood the field approach very well. Over a period of several years he had talked about various fields with his father and had pushed him gently toward music. In fact, it was partly under the influence of the son's gentle urging that John moved ahead with the small band. Again, it was the son who first suggested that the group play for the public. For all his randomness and delay, John Barton finally achieved a satisfactory style of life in retirement. In the absence of planning, most people I know are rarely as fortunate.

Robert and Marge Kurt

Sometimes, thoughtful planning leads a person into new and different activities in retirement—activities not directly related to the person's primary field of occupation before retirement. Such was the case with Robert.

One afternoon, Robert went to lunch with an old friend who was celebrating his sixtieth birthday. Robert also was 60 years old. His friend, who held a top executive position, announced that he was going to be fired. For a moment, Robert was shocked and incredulous, but then he realized it had to be a gag, because he knew his friend pretty well. When pressed, his friend said, "Well, I'll be 65 in five years, and I'm going to be retired whether I like it or not. They call it retirement, but I call it being fired." He also said that because he knew this was coming, he had already started to plan for the day when he would no longer have his position. As it turned out, this man retired technically but continued to be very active in the business world. He accepted directorships in a number of large corporations, assisted others in starting some new corporate ventures, and remained as busy as he had ever been.

During the birthday luncheon, it occurred to Robert for the first time that the age of 60 was none too soon to begin planning for retirement. Therefore, he started to make his own plans. A financial analysis indicated that Robert probably could live comfortably within his estimated retirement income. He decided that, if necessary, he would use some of his capital for extraordinary expenses, such as major travel or illness. It seemed only logical to Robert that if he lived long enough and could not increase his income as fast as inflation, he should be willing to use some of his capital to continue to live comfortably.

Robert did not consider changing his residence, because he had lived in the same area for over 30 years and had many long-standing friendships that were important to him. His wife, Marge, concurred in this because she was much involved in hospital work and social services in the area. After some years as director of social services in a large hospital, she had retired early and had become extremely active on boards and committees for child welfare, a program of activity that she wished to continue.

Unlike his wife, Robert was not at all sure how he wanted to spend his time in retirement. He undertook an active search for new, different, interesting activities. A preliminary analysis of his fields of interest led to the disclosure of several possibilities that seemed worth deeper exploration.

Gardening

He and Marge had achieved great satisfaction in planting and landscaping their place in the country. Over the years, they both had loved gardening and had enjoyed working on the grounds together. This was, in fact, a major hobby for both of them and was one of the reasons they wanted to maintain their home rather than live in a condominium. They relied on this outdoor activity for exercise, for neither was inclined toward sports. When their friends went to play golf or tennis, Robert and Marge preferred to work in the garden.

Travel

Robert had worked abroad and had traveled extensively for both business and pleasure. He and Marge looked forward to more leisurely trips. They even wanted to take a tent safari through East Africa. This was not a possibility while they were working full time, but they did realize this ambition after retirement.

Psychology

During the later years of his business career, Robert had been doing more and more personnel work. This had led him to read seriously in the field of psychology for the first time. He found psychology extremely interesting, and his readings increased his sense of competence in his work. He had taken an elementary course in psychology at night while still working.

Counseling

Robert included counseling on his list because of his interest in psychology and because he had been successful as a counselor in personnel work. Although he did not really intend to do more of the same in retirement, he felt that he should explore the field of counseling a bit further before making any decisions.

Research

Research-based management consulting had comprised a significant part of Robert's business life. He liked to do research and had many years of experience to bring to it.

After isolating these fields for more detailed consideration, Robert began to explore them systematically. Gardening, he realized, was a hobby and always would be only that. He had no ambition to make it a specialty or a business activity. Just working on his own place was fun. He came to the same conclusion about travel. He wasn't interested in being a travel agent or tour guide, or in working for a transportation company. He really wanted to stay on the receiving end of the travel business and to use it purely for pleasure. Like gardening, travel promised little in the way of satisfying work life but remained an important avocation.

Robert looked carefully at psychology and counseling and felt that he would like to continue to explore these interests. He even considered combining counseling with research. Even preliminary investigation indicated that he would need a better academic background in these subjects as a requirement for entry into the field. Robert had had a taste of adult education when he took a night course in elementary psychology, so he knew that it would not be too difficult for him to continue his studies successfully. Psychologically he had to consider adult education as a means to an end rather than as a long-term goal or end in itself.

He reviewed college catalogs and talked to professors in a number of graduate schools. Eventually, he applied to and was accepted for a master's program in psychology at Teachers College, Columbia University. Almost immediately upon enrolling, Robert was convinced that he had made the right choice. The field was fascinating and gave him a whole new set of contacts with young intellectuals. He enjoyed the stimulation of learning and felt a real challenge to do well academically.

Ironically, the most difficult part of it all turned out to be what Robert called the "newfangled" multiple-choice examinations, which he had never encountered in his earlier school days. He acknowledged that maybe he had trouble with these tests because his reflexes had slowed down just a bit, and the tests tended to emphasize speed at least as much as knowledge of the subject matter. Nevertheless, he received his degree.

Recognizing that his education was a means to an end, he decided not to go on for a doctorate, which would have taken at least another three years. Had he been career oriented, a Ph.D. would have been essential; but Robert just wanted to work at the things he liked, and to do so at his own pace. Now he had the credentials that were necessary for entry. To continue as a counselor came naturally once he had his master's degree. He had enough contacts and referrals to keep him as busy as he wanted to be.

Getting into research was a different kind of problem. He discovered that research grants generally were given to universities and were awarded almost exclusively to professors. Through intensive inquiry while he was still in school, Robert found out that his only route into research would be through establishing good personal relations with professors who had received grants. He set himself the goal of becoming an accepted member of a research group under the direction of a professor. He did secure such a position and at first was willing to accept any task given to him—usually something no one else wanted—until he could establish his position and his qualifications to do more interesting research work.

Throughout his planning and pursuit of affirmative retirement, Robert treated retirement not as an event, but as an ongoing process. It took him two years to get a master's degree and another three years working with a research group to reach a point where he was well accepted as a competent researcher. At 70 years of age, he looks forward to many more interesting and productive years.

I would like to add one closing note here. Years ago Alexander Woollcott had a popular radio program called *The Town Crier*. Fondly, I recall that once in a while he would do a biographical feature with a "snaperoo ending." That is, he would give a biography of some famous and interesting person without revealing the person's name until the very end. Sometimes the person's identity was obvious, and sometimes it came as a profound surprise to his listeners. I wrote this case study with the intention of concealing Robert's identity from you, but I later decided to ask his permission. Could I divulge his identity? "Why not?" he replied. "Everyone knows by this time that I practice what I preach. I am, after all, the author of this book."

6

Changing Threat to Promise

For many centuries, our civilization developed as a rural society based on agriculture, hunting, fishing, and trading. Life expectancy was well under 50 years, and there was no such thing as retirement.

Technology has brought radical changes in our way of living. Life expectancy, still increasing, is now over 70 years. We have become an urban rather than a rural society. Mobility has increased fantastically in the last 100 years with the advent of good roads, railroads, automobiles, and airplanes.

All these changes have been too rapid to permit our society to develop a new set of guidelines and disciplines for life in retirement. So far, society has succeeded only in alleviating some of the financial problems of retirement through pensions and social security. No attempt has been made to deal with psychological and social concerns. As a result, many retirees are frustrated and bewildered when they no longer have the disciplines that society previously imposed. There is, however, a favorable side. Fortunately for you who are leaving the workforce, you are now free to choose and develop your own individual destiny.

Now it is up to you to create your own case study. If you have followed the system outlined in this book, you should have all the preliminary materials you need. You may even be far enough along in your planning to notice a lessening of any tension you may have felt as you began Chapter 1. One natural and pleasant consequence of this kind of planning is that you can begin to look toward the future with a sense of possibility and purpose.

Right now, you probably know more about your financial circumstances than you have known for years. You have probably done more systematic thinking about your goals and satisfactions than you ever did before. Perhaps you have even made some preliminary decisions about how you will use your time after you leave your job. Now you have a sense of moving *toward* something, and that is the antidote for the sense of tension and dread that often attend an unplanned retirement.

Your job is not finished. It is not easy to establish harmony among your financial, personal, and social objectives, but *it can be done.* If you do not know all the answers yet, please rest assured that that is to be expected. Be assured also that if you continue to work within this system, you will eventually find solutions.

Furthermore, even if you think that you already have some answers, be forewarned that you will be tempted to modify your solutions as time goes on. The conditions and preferences of retirement change, for people themselves evolve over time. You should be prepared to go through the planning process again at a later date, if only to check your initial decisions. You can readily make up your own set of worksheets from the samples shown in the relevant chapters.

The most common problem at the end of this first round of planning is that people find themselves with more ambitions than they can carry out. You may have noticed that there are simply too many interesting possibilities available to you, and you know that you cannot do them all. Instead of feeling unhappy about that, just consider how miserable you would be if you had no focus at all—no thrust toward the future. Count yourself lucky to be among those who have realized that retirement does not mean a retreat from everything, that it is merely a withdrawal from traditional working life. Retirement from the job is an important milestone, and it should not be taken lightly; but neither should it become equated with the end of life, happiness, and productivity. In the promise of new activities lies an end to the threat of turning 65.

Some years ago, one of my clients went through the planning system outlined in this book and derived from it some forceful and highly motivating ambitions for his retirement years. He was obviously pleased with the results, so I was a little taken aback when he told me that he had a major complaint. Then he explained, "Bob, this was extremely useful to me, but I can't help thinking that I could have used it when I was 40 years old. It isn't just a retirement-planning system, you know. It is a way to analyze the pos-

sibilities and figure out your goals at any stage of life."
What he said is true, of course. Many of the techniques
in this book can be used to clarify people's ambitions
at any stage of life. I would be willing to bet that you
are now in a better position to discuss goals with
younger people than you ever were before.

Index